A Guide to
Jewish Genealogy in
Latvia and Estonia

No. 8 in the Jewish Ancestor Series

by

Arlene Beare

JGSGB Latvian Special Interest Group

זכר ימות עולם בינו שנות דר-ודר
שאל אביך ויגדך זקניך ויאמרו-לך :
Remember the days of old, consider the years of many generations:
Ask thy father, and he will declare unto thee: Thine elders and they will tell thee.
Deuteronomy XXX11 v.7   דברים לב ז

1

Published by
The Jewish Genealogical Society of Great Britain
Registered Charity No. 1022738
JGSGB Publications, PO Box 180, St. Albans,
Herts. AL2 3WH. England U.K.
E-mail: publications@jgsgb.org.uk
Web-site: www.jgsgb.org.uk

First edition March 2001
Second Edition June 2006

Copyright © Arlene Beare

ISBN: 0-9537669-9-3

Front cover designed by
Rosemary Hoffman and Derek Wenzerul

Printed and bound in the United Kingdom
by the Alden Group Ltd., Oxford
☎ 01865 253200

The information contained in the Guide is believed to be accurate at the time of printing. However, information can become out-of-date. This Guide is sold on the condition that neither the Authors nor the Society can be held legally responsible for the consequences of any errors or omissions that there may be.

CONTENTS

Part II: ESTONIA

4

JEWISH GENEALOGICAL SOCIETY OF GREAT BRITAIN (JGSGB)

The JGSGB is the premier society for Jewish genealogy in Great Britain. The Society encourages genealogical research and promotes the preservation of Jewish genealogical records and resources. It provides a forum for sharing information amongst members.membership is open to both beginners and to more experienced researchers. Members have the opportunity to meet like-minded people at central meetings, regional meetings, (East London, Leeds, Manchester, Oxford, South Coast, and South-West London), group meetings and at informal meetings in members' homes.

GENERAL ENQUIRIES
E-mail: enquiries@jgsgb.org.uk
Web-site: <www.jgsgb.org.uk>
MEMBERSHIP ENQUIRIES
The Membership Secretary,
PO Box 2508, Maidenhead, SL6 8WS. England, U.K.
E-mail: membership@jgsgb.org.uk
PUBLICATIONS
JGSGB Publications,
PO Box 180, St. Albans, Herts. AL2 3WH. England, U.K.
E-mail: publications@jgsgb.org.uk

MEMBERS' GENEALOGICAL RESOURCE LIBRARY
The library contains extensive information and genealogical resources including several hundred reference books, computers and a selection of genealogical CD-ROMs and other genealogical databases. IT helpers are on hand to assist. It also houses a large collection of maps and leaflets as well as microfilms and microfiches (including copies of many of the major Anglo-Jewish genealogy collections).

WEB-SITE
Our Web-site <www.jgsgb.org.uk> has a resource-packed section reserved for JGSGB members only and links to almost every conceivable genealogical Web-site.

JGSGB JOURNAL
Shemot is the Journal of The Jewish Genealogical Society of Great Britain. It is published quarterly and is free to members of the Society. If you are trying to trace *Shemot* in a public library, it may help to quote the international reference number ISSN 0969-2258.

FOREWORD

This publication is part of the *Jewish Ancestors* series of booklets produced by the Jewish Genealogical Society of Great Britain (JGSGB). Its intention is to point in the right direction our members and others who are researching their families in the UK and in Latvia and Estonia.

This guide, as with others in the series, is only an introduction to genealogy and is not totally comprehensive. There are many other references that must be consulted as one makes progress with one's research. It is not always easy to determine what should be included and I have tried to select information that I feel will be of help to the novice as well as to the experienced researcher.

I have endeavoured to enlarge the scope of this book by adding more detailed information on emigration and passports. The expanded Emigration section includes an extract from a paper on "Libau and Port Jews" by Nicholas J. Evans and a summary of a paper by Irina Weinberga on Passport control in the Russian Empire.

In order to answer the queries of many researchers I have included a FAQs (Frequently Asked Questions) section. This will facilitate your search for information that is most relevant to your needs.

The tremendous cooperation that Latvian researchers have received from the Latvian State Historical archivists must be mentioned. Details of how to contact the Archive and request a search can be found in the text. There is an update of the account details that you will receive from the Archives and the English translation will enable you to see how you have been billed.

The growth of information on the Internet has provided a wealth of material on genealogical topics and I have indicated how computers may be of help. Archival sources remain the definitive source for documenting and verifying data.

Important information on new databases that have been added to the Jewishgen Latvia Database formerly known as the All Latvia Database are included as well as a more detailed section on sightseeing in Riga. A list of Jewish firms in Riga in 1891 has many surnames and addresses that will be of great interest.

You will find contact details for the Association of Latvian and Estonians in Israel.

I have also tried to explain how to broaden the search and not remain restricted to one shtetl or one country of origin. Our ancestors were an itinerant people making research both interesting and difficult.

Arlene Beare
Archive Representative for Latvia SIG
JGSGB Latvian Special Interest Group

Arlene Beare (Past President of Latvia SIG hosted by Jewishgen) has worked unbelievably hard and shown tremendous enthusiasm writing and updating this publication. The JGSGB Guide to Jewish Genealogy in Latvia and Estonia was the first of its kind and with Arlene's experience and expertise in this field will continue to be an invaluable source of information for those researching in this area.

Rosemary Wenzerul
Chairman, JGSGB Publications Committee
Member of Council
June 2006

ACKNOWLEDGEMENTS

Rosemary Wenzerul has helped greatly with the preparation of this Guide. She works with total commitment and her experience in publishing the JGSGB Introductory Guides has been invaluable. I thank **Derek Wenzerul** for help with the computer layouts for printing and am very grateful to **Lydia Collins** for proof reading the final draft.

I acknowledge the following contributions to the first edition:
David Fielker (past editor of the JGSGB journal, *Shemot*) brought his expertise to the editing of the final draft.
Cyril Fox helped with the bibliography and **Derek Wenzerul** assisted with miscellaneous computing problems. **Rosemary Wenzerul** contributed the sections on the Latvian and Estonian languages.
Marion Werle, with her extensive knowledge of Latvian genealogy, read and commented incisively on portions of the text and compiled the original Latvian bibliography. **Nick Evans** provided invaluable information on emigration. **Constance Whippman** contributed the history of Courland, as well as excellent introductions to the databases and the acquisitions of the Courland Research Group.
Prof Ruvin Ferber of the Centre for Judaic Studies at the University of Latvia and the archivists at the Latvian State Historical Archives, in particular **Rita Bogdanova**, checked data information and provided helpful comments. **Vadim Altskan** of the United States Holocaust Memorial Museum contributed data on the Holocaust in Latvia.
Contributions on Estonia came from **Len Yodaiken**, **Adam Katzeff**, **Tatjana Schor** (University of Tartu) and **Ken Kalling** (Museum University of Tartu). Publications by **Aivars Stranga** provided helpful information.
Saul Issroff (JGSGB Lithuanian Expert) read the final draft of the first edition and made helpful comments.

PART I
LATVIA

History

Latvia is one of the Baltic States and is located on the Baltic Sea across the water from Sweden. Other Baltic States are Estonia, Lithuania and Poland. Present-day Latvia is divided into four regions - **Kurzeme, Zemgale, Vidzeme** and **Latgale**. see map on page 10.

Kurzeme in the north-west and **Zemgale** in the south-west are regions that were previously named Courland (Kurland). The river Dvina separates them from Vidzeme. Courland was part of the Russian Empire after the Third Partition of Poland. In the 1870's many Lithuanians migrated into Courland. There was also at that time a large migration into Latvia from Poland, Belarus and the Ukraine.

Vidzeme which was known as Livonia (Lifland) extends from Riga to Estonia. Northern Latvia was called Riga Province until 1783 and became Lifland in 1796. Parts of Lifland are now in Estonia.

Latgale in modern Latvia is the region in the south-east. Poland and Lithuania were a Commonwealth from 1569 and Latgale was part of this Commonwealth. It was known as "Inflantia" or "Polish Livonia". Russia extended its boundaries westwards with the three partitions of Poland 1772, 1792 and 1795. After the Third Partition of Poland in 1795 Latgale became part of Vitebsk Province in the Russian Empire. Some of the shtetlach (townlets) that belonged to Vitebsk until 1917 are in Latgale, e.g. Ludza (Lutsin), Rēzekne (Rezhitsa) and Daugavpils (Dvinsk). In 1917 after the Revolution Latgale once more became part of Latvia.

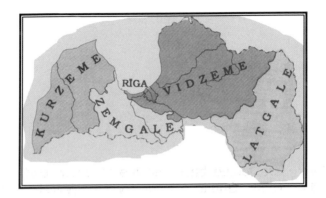

Riga

Riga was founded in 1201 by the Teutonic Order. Jews have lived in Latvia for many centuries under German (the Teutonic Knights), Polish, Prussian, Swedish and Danish rule. They originated from Germany, Lithuania and Russia and from other countries. Jewish history in the tiny shtetlach dates back to the 15th century and possibly even to the 10th century.

Jews were allowed to come to Riga to work for limited periods of time but could not live in the city permanently. In 1638 a hostel was opened for them and in 1725 they received permission to establish a Jewish cemetery. There were about 70 Jews in Riga at this time and they left in 1743 when the Jews of Russia were banished. In 1764 some rich Jewish families were classed as 'protected Jews' and were considered as guardians of the 'foreign Jews' who had come to the hostel. In 1765 a chevra kadisha (burial society) was officially founded. Riga, Livonia and Courland were never part of the Pale of Settlement. The Jewish community comprised two groups. One originated in Courland and the dominant culture was German. The second group, mainly Hasidim, came from Minsk, Vitebsk and White Russia.

In 1785 Jews traded in Riga but had to register in a small town called Sloka (Schlock) not far away. In 1813 they were granted permission to live in Riga and there were 736 inhabitants, comprising protected Jews, foreign Jews and Schlock citizens. In 1858 they were allowed to own real estate. The area around Moscow Road was known as 'Moscow Vorstadt' and was a main area of Jewish settlement. At the end of the 19th century some Jews moved out and lived in the centre of the city.

In 1941 they were forced back into the Moscow road area, which became the Riga Ghetto. There were Jewish intellectuals, professionals and tradesmen but between the two World Wars about 10% of Latvian Jews were paupers. In 1915 the Germans invaded Courland (Kurland), drove all Jews from their houses and deported them to Russia. Some Riga Jews went with their deported relations. In 1940-1941 leading Jews were arrested and perished in Stalin's Gulag. The KGB deported 14,000 inhabitants of Latvia on 14 June 1941, including about 5,000 Jews, half of them from Riga. After the war some survivors returned and some Jews from the USSR settled in Riga. 23,000 Jews were registered in 1989. There are at present about 9,000 Jews in Latvia. Sadly this number is diminishing as many Jews emigrate to Israel, USA and Europe. [1]

Daugavpils [2] (Dvinsk)
Daugavpils is one of the largest towns in Latvia after Riga and is situated on the Daugava (Dvina) river, which travels from its origins near the Volga through Vitebsk, Polotsk, Daugavpils (Dvinsk) and Jekabpils (Jakobstadt), flowing over 600 miles to Riga and the Baltic. Jews moved to Dvinsk from Poland and Lithuania in the 17th century, but Jewish burials in the 16th century were recorded at an old cemetery in the Alstadt neighbourhood.

The Jewish population of Dvinsk grew rapidly after its inclusion in the Pale, exceeding 30,000 by 1900. It was an important railway centre midway between St Petersburg and Warsaw with a line to Libau. At the end of the 19th century these important links of river and rail were integral to attracting a Jewish presence.

Trades in timber, leather and flax were important economic activities. Literacy in Yiddish was high, trade schools were established, and the study of the Talmud was widespread. The majority of Jews were merchants and 40% practised as craftsmen. These factors would draw individuals and families from neighbouring Belarus (Byelorussia) and the adjacent borders of today's Lithuania in search of opportunity and improvement. A synagogue built in 1928 still exists and services are held daily. There are fewer than 800 Jews there today. The synagogue has data on Jews dating from the 1930s.

Rēzekne
Jews settled in Rēzekne in the late 18th century. A hundred years ago there were about 6,500 Jews living in Rēzekne but this had reduced to 3,342 in 1935. Only 120 Jews were living there in June 1999. Most of the community are old and sick and need assistance. Ten pupils attend Jewish instruction on Sunday. The synagogue was built in 1845 and the roof has been destroyed. There are no services.

Liepāja
Jews were allowed to live in Liepāja from 1799. Liepāja was an important Baltic port from which many of our ancestors left Latvia. In 1835 a new Code was published allowing permanent residence to the Jews living there with their families and registered locally according to the last census of the population. 400 Jewish families were expelled in 1890. Although the prevailing culture was German many Jews remained loyal to their traditions and the Yiddish language. The Germans invaded in June 1941 and on the 13 December there was a mass *Aktion*. All the Jews apart from approximately 1000 were taken to Skede and executed by firing squads. Over a period of 3 days about 2,800 lost their lives. The Jews were confined to a Ghetto in July 1942. The Ghetto was liquidated in October 1943 and the Jews were transferred to Kaiserwald concentration camp near Riga. See memorial photos pages 102 and 104.

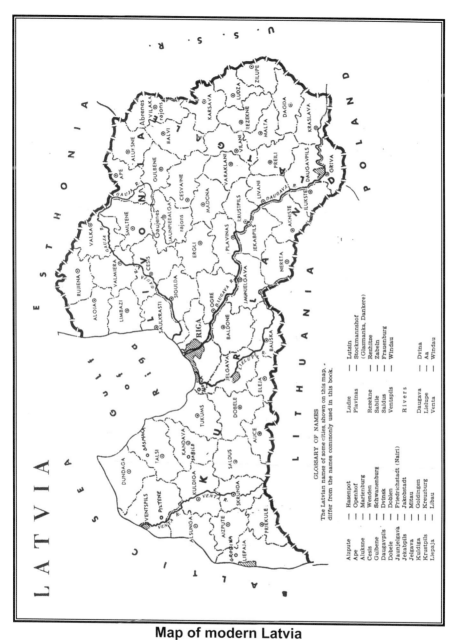

Map of modern Latvia
Printed with permission from The Association of Latvian and Estonian
Jews, Kibbutz Shefayim, Israel

13

Courland (Kurland) [3]

Courland is the historic name of the area, which was situated between Kovno gubernia (now Lithuania) and the Dvina (now Daugava) river. The native tribal inhabitants were subjected to a brutal campaign of forced Christianisation (the Baltic Crusades) in the 12th century, spearheaded by the Germans and Prussians, and it was ruled as a theocracy until 1561. From then until the late 18th century Courland functioned as a duchy, headed by the Duke of Courland, a dynasty descending from the last of the Grand Masters of the previous religious order. In 1795 the Duchy was formally absorbed by Russia under the third partition of Poland. From 1795 to 1918 Courland existed as a separate German-speaking province (gubernia) of the Russian Empire with its capital at Mitau (now Jelgava). Jews were legally allowed to settle in the areas of Courland controlled by the Bishop of Piltene until 1834, and on a more restricted basis after that date. Courland remained outside the Pale of Settlement and escaped the worst of the oppressions and hardships suffered by the Jews in the Pale.

Evidence of Jewish settlement in the form of gravestones near Jelgava has been identified dating from around the 15th century. In most Courland towns the Jewish community made up the majority of small business owners and were involved in a significant proportion of the major industrial enterprises. Sporadic attempts were made to restrict later emigration, which nonetheless continued at a high level, particularly from Lithuania, and to a lesser extent from Belarus in the latter half of the 19th century.

The Jewish population of Courland was severely affected by efforts to expel them to the interior areas of Russia in 1915 because of the dislocation caused by World War I and suspicions about their loyalty to the German forces. Following the War the Jewish community returned, at least in part.

The All Russian Census of 1897 records some 51,072 Jews living in Courland. It was not until the 1890s that the use of Russian was made mandatory in public documents; nevertheless the use of German remained widespread and the Russian authorities and the Baltic German ruling class ruled throughout the area co-operatively.

Courland was ruled by the Baltic Germans and the administration of the area remained subject to Baltic German control even after its absorption into the Russian Empire following the 3rd Partition of Poland. German [or Latin during the very earliest period] was the language of administration and high culture for nearly 700 years and was only gradually displaced by Russian and Latvian in the late 19th and early 20th century. Courland was the only German speaking Gubernia in the Russian Empire and remained so until the final thrust of Russification was complete in or about the 1890s. Even then clear remnants of its German past were retained.

The principal ports of emigration were Liepāja (Libau) and Ventspils (Windau). These were able to operate all year round because they remained largely ice-free throughout the winter months. Riga also had a share in the emigration traffic, but to a lesser extent because its location meant that it was at continual risk of being ice-bound from November until March or April. There was a strong Zionist movement from the late 18th century onwards and many Courland families tried their fortune as part of the agricultural colonies movement migrating to the interior of the Empire.

It is estimated that approximately 50-60% of the Jewish residents of Riga had their roots in Courland, so that searching Courland material often pays dividends for those whose last place of known family contact is said to be 'Riga'. Similarly the major centres of Jewish population in Dvinsk were only a few kilometres from Courland and many families find that previous generations had links to Courland.

STARTING YOUR RESEARCH

Where do you begin?

You are reading this book because you have embarked on the exciting trail of discovery to know more about your ancestors, how they lived and how they died. The search will be rewarding if you apply yourself with diligence, as you will meet with many obstacles on the way. You will need to follow all clues and write many letters. If you join your local genealogical society you will find well-informed researchers to help you with advice and guidance. Addresses of record repositories in the UK will be detailed below; however, you will find similar repositories if you live in another country. This booklet is an introduction, and more comprehensive information will be found in other sources. However it should be of assistance to you no matter where your ancestors came from in the Russian Empire. Sources in the Latvian State Historical Archives will mirror closely the documents found in other Archives in the Russian Empire such as Lithuania and Belarus.

Acquire as much information on your **family** as possible. Ask all living ancestors for information on their family history. Important details you require are family names (including original surnames), dates of birth, marriage and death, the name of the shtetl they were born in (if known), the one lived in and the one they left from if they emigrated.

The **shtetl** name that you have may be the one that you remember from discussion with your parents or other relations. Genealogical research requires that you use the contemporary name when looking for details on the shtetl of origin. This can be found in the index of any standard atlas. You can also consult the revised edition of the book *Where Once We Walked* by Gary Mokotoff and Sallyann Amdur Sack in which, with a few exceptions, you will find the contemporary Latvian name as well as older names. Order from their webpage: <http://www.avotaynu.com> Take care to expand your search; our ancestors often remained as taxpayers in their shtetl of origin, so you may be disappointed if you research only in one area. Many Latvians, for instance, originated in Lithuania and continued to pay taxes there.

The Russian Empire was divided into Provinces (**Gubernias**) and these were divided into Districts (**Uyezdy**). Another common problem is that the name of the **shtetl** may be the same as the district; for example, there is the district of Daugavpils (Dvinsk) and a town of Daugavpils (Dvinsk). An ancestor reputed to come from Daugavpils (Dvinsk) might in fact have come from any of the shtetlach in the district. For example Gostini and Dagda were in the district of Daugavpils (Dvinsk) and in the Province (Gubernia) of Vitebsk.

See **Inventory of Holdings in Latvian State Historical Archives** for details of shtetl, district and province names.
Webpage:
<http://www.shtetlinks.Jewishgen.org/riga/rigapage.htm>.

Surnames were taken at different times in different countries. Austrian Empire (1787), Russian Pale (1804, not enforced until 1835/1845), Russian Poland (1821), West Galicia (1805), France (1808), and in various German states: Frankfurt (1807), Baden (1809), Westphalia (1812), Prussia (1812), Bavaria (1813), Wuerttemberg (1828), Posen (1833), Saxony (1834).

Prior to the 18th century most Jews used patronymics, e.g. Avram ben Yankel (Avram son of Yankel). When you took a surname, in general the lower down in the social order you were, the more likely you were to take a name of the town you were living in or the name of your trade, e.g. Dorfman or Schneider.
Sephardic surnames date back to the 1500s. Ashkenazi surnames in general date from the end of the 18th century. Some German Jews had surnames as early as the Middle Ages. The choice was left to the individual Jews, but at the end of the 18th century, for purposes of taxation and conscription, laws required that all Jews had surnames.
On 9 December 1804, Czar Alexander I issued an Imperial Statute "Concerning the Organisation of Jews". A partial translation of Article 32 reads: 'Every Jew must have or adopt an inherited last name, or nickname, which should be used in all official acts and records without change.'

Alexander Beider, an expert in Russian-Jewish family names, has pointed out that the law was not rigorously observed. On 31 May 1835, Nicholas I issued another Imperial Statute concerning the Jews. A translation of Article 16 reads: 'Every Jew, in addition to a first name given at a profession of faith or birth, must forever retain, without alteration, a known inherited or legally adopted surname or nickname.' [4]

For further information on Jewish naming patterns read
Beider, Alexander, A *Dictionary of Jewish Surnames from the Russian Empire*, Teaneck NJ, Avotaynu Inc,1993.

SOURCES OF INFORMATION

Records that will be of assistance to you in your own country:
vital records (births, marriages and deaths)
naturalisation records
wills and probate records
newspaper entries
school records
passport applications
passenger lists
military records
criminal records
trade directories
synagogue records
cemetery records

Research Sources in the UK

The principles involved in searching are the same in each country and you will need to get corresponding addresses for repositories in your country if you live elsewhere.

If you live in the UK you may wish to consult the Society's *A Guide to Jewish Genealogy in the United Kingdom,* ISBN: 0 9537669 7 7 which gives details of available resources in the UK. This publication gives greater detail of available resources.

Start with **vital** records (births, marriages and deaths)

Family Records Centre (FRC)
1 Myddelton Street, London EC1R 1UW
Tel: 0845 603 7788   Fax: 01704 550013
E-mail: certificate.services@ons.gsi.gov.uk

For Census and general enquiries (not B,M,D)
Tel: 020 8392 5300 Fax: 020 8487 9214
E-mail: frc@nationalarchives.gov.uk
Web-site: <www.familyrecords.gov.uk/frc/default.htm>

If you are unable to visit the FRC then you should write to:
General Register Office,
PO Box 2, Southport, Merseyside, PR8 2JD.
Tel: 0845 603 7788
E-mail: certificate.services@ons.gsi.gov.uk
Web-site: <www.statistics.gov.uk/registration>

When trying to find a birth, marriage or death record it is important to remember that civil registration of births in England and Wales only began in 1837, and at that time you did not have to give a name. Prior to 1837 registers were in the hands of the religious authorities but some indexes are available at the National Archives. A penalty for non-registration was introduced from 1874. Sometimes the birth would be registered under the surname of the mother so remember to check under her name if you cannot find it under the father's surname. Note the reference from the index as you will need it to complete the appropriate form. A fee is charged and the certificate can be posted to you.

The National Archives formerly the Public Record Office
Ruskin Avenue, Kew, Surrey TW9 4DU
Tel: 020 8876 3444 Fax: 020 8392 5286
Web-site: <www.nationalarchives.gov.uk>

Marriage certificates give the name of the father and his occupation. The age at the time of the marriage may help but often the correct age was not given. The names of witnesses may be useful as they were often close members of the family

The National Archives (PRO) holds listings for **naturalisations** in the Home Office records. If your ancestor applied for naturalisation there were usually two letters of recommendation required and these often provided a wealth of background information.

The National Archives **passenger lists** for 1890-1960 outwards are in BT 27, (Board of Trade) listed under year of departure, so it may help if the year of entry is known but the lists are not easily accessed. Arrivals 1878-1888 and 1890-1960 are in BT 26. These lists are not indexed. There is a current project proposal to get them into database format.

For further information on passenger lists see page 58

Some **school records** are held at:
London Metropolitan Archives
40 Northampton Road, London EC1R OHB
Tel: 020 7332 3820 - Fax: 020 7833 9136
Among other records they have records of the Jews' Free School.

Wills are a very useful source of information and can be found at:
Principal Registry of the Family Division
1st Avenue House, 42-49 High Holborn, London W1V 6NP
Tel: 020 7936 6000 and 020 7936 6801

Newspapers such as the *Jewish Chronicle* contain announcements of births, marriages and deaths.
Jewish Chronicle Library
25 Furnival Street, London, EC4A 1JT
Tel: 020 7415 1500
An appointment is necessary

The Mormons (Church of Jesus Christ of Latter Day Saints-LDS) have the largest collection of **genealogical records** in the world. Their address in London is:
Family History Centre,
Church of Jesus Christ of Latter Day Saints,
64-68 Exhibition Road, South Kensington, London SW7 2PA
Tel: 020 7589 8561
(Family History Support Office: 0121 384 2028 for opening times of all Family History Centres)
Jewish researchers are amazed to find that the LDS hold such a large collection of Jewish records. A pamphlet detailing them can be obtained from any LDS centre. There are centres in many cities. Films not in stock can be ordered from Salt Lake City for a fee. The Library's catalogue is also available for purchase on CD.
The Web site is: <http://www.familysearch.org>

Israel

Records of the Association of Latvian and Estonian Jews
The Association of Latvian and Estonian Jews keeps a set of records at Kibbutz Shefayim describing many aspects of Jewish life in Latvia and Estonia. The listing of documents held in the archives has been a project undertaken by the late Schlomo Kurlandchik, archivist and advocate, and Dr Martha Lev-Zion historian. Martha Lev-Zion has compiled an inventory of the town records which is available online on the Riga page as well as the Courland Research Group page.

<http://www.shtetlinks.Jewishgen.org/riga/ShefayimT1.htm>

The Courland Research group link has additional information on the holdings of the Archive.
<http://www.Jewishgen.org/Courland/data_by_sources.htm#shefayim>

The records have been indexed under headings such as:Latvian Jewish personalities; Latvian Jewish organisations, parties, institutions and movements; photos of Latvian Jewish personalities; and photos of Latvian Jewish organisations.

Details of the Shefayim Archive taken from their Webpage

Archives of the Association of Latvian & Estonian Jews in Israel
Educational Center, Hof Hasharon, Shefayim 60990
Tel: 972 9 9596532
Fax: 972 9 9552848
E-mail: iygal@netvision.net.il
Website:
<http://www.Jewishgen.org/Courland/data_by_sources.htm#shefayim>

Archivists: Yitzhak Gal (Hebrew, English, Yiddish, German)
Jacob Golan (Hebrew, English, Russian, Yiddish)
Ezra Tov (Hebrew, English, Russian, Yiddish)

Hours of Operation: Monday 14:00-17:00, Tuesday 10:00-13:00
Consultation: An appointment is needed.
Closest Public Transportation:
Bus: Bus 601 Tel-Aviv-Netanya
Directions: By car take Tel Aviv Netanya Highway, 10 km. North of
Tel Aviv
Access for Disabled: Yes
One should call or send an email rather than just arriving because
they will open on other days if need be. On occasions they have
doctor's appointments or other commitments and are not able to
come at the advertised hour. Contact should always be made first.

The material appears in the following languages: Hebrew, English,
Russian, Yiddish, Latvian and German. The family trees are in
manuscript form. There are books on various Jewish communities
and oral testimonies in manuscript form. There are also photos and
books of genealogical interest. The catalogue is computerized and in
English. It can be accessed from the website. The materials are
located in locked steel closets.

Searches can be made from abroad for a charge of $20 per search
and $0.20 for each document.

RESEARCH SOURCES IN LATVIA

Latvian State Historical Archives
Before doing overseas research, it is essential that you first exhaust all resources available domestically. The more information you have, the greater your chances of success with an overseas inquiry. Once you have your basic information you should write to:
Latvian State Historical Archives
16, Slokas Str., Riga LV-1007, Latvia
Tel: +371 7 614008 - Fax: +371 7 612406
Chief Archivist: Mrs Irina Veinberga
Email: irinwin@latnet.lv
Assistant archivists: Mrs Jelena Polovceva, Ms Rita Bogdanova.

Your letter can be written in English and should include as much detail as possible about your family (names, ages, etc) and should indicate the specific town where your family originated, since most records are arranged by locality.

Be sure to use the names they had in their place of origin, not the Anglicised versions (e.g., Moshe not Morris, Ber not Barnett). It is not necessary to send money with the initial request to the Archive.

If the Archivists feel they can do research for you they will notify you, in English, of the non-refundable deposit that is required. At the time of writing the deposit asked for is a postal order (money order) to the value of $100 or the equivalent currency (add US$7 for bank charges if sending a cheque). There can be a delay of from six months to a year for results.

A complete inventory of the holdings of the Archives may be found at: <http://www.shtetlinks.Jewishgen.org/riga/rigapage.htm> click link. Note that this inventory has no names but details what lists are held in the archives.

Account from Archives in Latvian [5]

Pamat ojums	Pakalpojuma veids	Mervien	Cena Ls	Skaits	Kopa	Val
1.3.3.	Dokumentu apzinasana					
1.3.3.1.	masinraksta, salasama rokraksta	1 gl.v.	1.31			
1.3.3.2.	salasams teksts ar paleografiskam ipatnibam	1 gl.v.	1.75			
1.3.3.3.	gruti salasams, dziestoss	1 gl.v.	2.62			
1.3.3.4.	lietu papildus izskatisana	1 gl.v.	0.54			
1.6.	Genealogiska petijuma sastadisana					
	par vienu personu (ar 3 ierakstiem par dzimsanu,	persona	10.54			
	par vienu personu ar 2 ierakstiem	persona	7.03			
	par vienu personu ar 1	persona	3.51			
1.9.3.	Negativas atbilde	izzina	0.75			
1.20	Sagatavotas izzinas tulkosana svesvaloda	A-4	5.29			
2.5.	Lietu izsniegsana no glabatavas					
2.5.1.	Lietas par periodu no 18.	1 gl.v.	0.105			
2.5.2.	Unikalas un lielformata lietas par periodu lidz 18.	1 gl.v.	0.17			
2.5.4	Apraksti	apraksts	0.13			
2.6.	Arhiva izzinas un tabulas	A-4	0.35			
2.7	Nodrukato tekstu					
2.7.1	originals masinraksta	A-4	0.32			
6.7	Kopesanas pakalpojumi	lappuse	0.80			
6.8	Dokumentu skanesana	lapa	1.31			
6.11	Skaneto dokumentu izdruka	lapa	1.03			
	Total					
15.	Vienosanas par koeficientu	koefic.				

English translation of Account

1.3.3.	Files examination		Ls
1.3.3.1.	Typewriting, a good handwriting	1 file	1.31
1.3.3.2.	A good handwriting difficult to read	1 file	1.75
1.3.3.3.	Missing text, difficult to read	1 file	2.62
1.3.3.4.	Additional files examination	1 file	0.54
1.6.	Genealogical research:		
	- one person (three entries) bmd	Person	10.54
	- one person (two entries)	Person	7.03
	- one person (one entry)	Person	3.51
1.9.3.	Negative answer	Report	0.75
1.20	Translation of reference	1 sheet	5.29
2.5.	To take and return files to depository		
2.5.1.	Files from the 18th century	1 file	0.105
2.5.2.	Unique and large format files	1 file	0.17
2.5.4	Inventories	1	0.13
2.6.	Typing of reference and table	1 sheet	0.35
2.7	Typed text editing		
2.7.1	Original typed	1 sheet	0.32
6.7	Copying of documents	1 sheet	0.80
6.8	Scanning of documents	1 sheet	1.31
6.11	Printing of scans	1 sheet	1.03
	Total		
15	Rate	Rate	
	VAT 18%		
	Total		
	Postal Expense		
	Total		
	Advanced payment		
	Total		
	Return to Researcher		

Records that will be searched by the archivists in Latvia:

Vital Records
Revision Lists
Recruits Enlistments Registers
Census Returns
Family Lists
Inhabitants Lists
Passport Registration Books
Passport issuing books
House Registers

Jewish Community Records date mainly from the 19th century but some date from the beginning of the 18th century.

Vital Records Jewish vital records (Births, Marriages and Deaths) are held from 1854 (the year they started to be kept officially) up to 1905, and a few beyond these dates. Some records have also been found that date back to 1811. Some books for the period 1890-1917 are in local registry offices but many are missing. Some books kept in the fonds of state facilities were destroyed because of lack of use. Prior to 1917 the governor's office or the office of the police in each major city in the Pale of Settlement kept one copy of Jewish vital records. Many of these were destroyed after a few years. Availability of vital records varies greatly, depending on the locale and the time period.

Unfortunately there are communities, where the vital records have been lost such as Kuldiga, Friedrichstadt and Talsen. Some have survived incompletely such as communities of Pilten, Rēzekne, Mitau, Ludza and Dvinsk. The fact that the Jewish vital records were kept in duplicate – one in the rabbinate and the second one in the police department has been helpful as at least one of them has survived and may be found in the documents of the police department. The vital records were compiled in Russian-Hebrew or in German-Hebrew.

Marriage Records include information on the ketubah. Russian and Hebrew entries may differ. The Hebrew is more complete and gives greater detail. Divorce records include the Rite of Halitza. 1850 -1860 records are more detailed as regards the cause of the divorce eg unable to have children.

Death Records help establish the birth date in cases where the birth records are not available.

Revision Lists (Reviskaya Schazka) which are like our Census returns were taken in different years. The Archives keep the revision lists from 1799 till 1858 and some additional lists till 1913. The last important revision was in 1858 - the 10th Revision. It recorded how many individuals were in a family at the time of the preceding revision and how many had left.

The early Revision Lists may not have surnames and were compiled in German. In rare cases they are in Russian. Russian became the official state language in 1892 in the records office and the All Russian Census is in Russian except for some towns in Courland, which are in German.

The most complete lists are for Riga, Mitau and Tukums and the least complete are for Latgale. Most records, however, are from the 8th Revision in 1834. These lists are complete for the towns of Jelgava, Liepāja and Tukums; incomplete lists are held for Jaunjelgava, Jekabpils, Kuldīga, Piltene and Ventspils. There are no revision lists for Aizpute and Bauska apart from a few pages of householders' lists for 1834.

Only certain information was recorded in the Revision Lists because the purpose of the revisions was to register the individuals in specific locations for taxation and military service. Names and ages of all males in the town were entered on one page, with names and ages of females opposite.

Recruits Enlistment Registers were constantly updated for military reasons. They are of great importance where Revision Lists have not survived eg Aizpute, Friedrichstadt and Goldingen. Lists that have survived for Courland are 1835,1842,1854,1868 and 1871. The list for Dvinsk for 1876 contains information on families from Preili, Glazmanka, Vishki and Kraslava. The Latvia Database has almost all the data on Recruits Enlistment. There are fonds about military service for the years 1874-1917 which have lists of recruits. In some lists there are details of the whole family, such as relationships and age. The Russian State Archives for Military History is the only archive that has records for the Czar's army prior to 1917. The exact name of the regiment or sub-unit has to be known in order to request information.

Conscription In 1827, personal military duty for Jews was first introduced in Russia, with recruits being from 12 to 25 years of age. However, although Jews were permitted to serve in the military, rights for having done so were not granted to them until 1856. For example, prior to 1856, a 25 year non-Jewish veteran would be given land, though it might be in an inaccessible place. In 1856, Jewish veterans also became eligible to receive land for their 25 years of military service. Special rights were given to converts. The Cantonist tragedy occurred in which children as young as 8 from the poorest homes were seized and deported to Kazan, Perm and Siberia. Many died as they were abandoned en route. In 1853 the Jews began seizing all Jews within their Districts who belonged to other Jewish communities to make up the quotas. You may wish to read a book called *The Cantonists - The Jewish Children's Army of the Tsar*, by Larry Dominitch, Devora Publishing, 2003

The **All Russian Census for 1897** is one of the best sources for 19th century Russian-Jewish genealogical research. Its aim was broader than for the revision lists, and information was collected about demographic composition, education, languages, literacy, occupation and religion. Details are given of family name, given name, father's name, sex, relationship to the head of the family, age, family status, estate, birth place, place of origin, place of abode, religion, native tongue, literacy, education, principal occupation and secondary occupations. Some 1897 lists are missing. It takes a great deal of time to find a family as the lists are not in alphabetic order but are listed by address. 1897 census details for a number of Towns are in the Latvia Database see page 76.

1	2	3	4	5	6	7	8
ФАМИЛІЯ (прозвище), ИМЯ и ОТЧЕСТВО или ИМЕНА, если ихъ нѣсколько. Отмѣтка о тѣхъ, кто окажется: слѣпымъ на оба глаза, нѣмымъ, глухонѣмымъ или умалишеннымъ.	Всѣ. М-муж-ской. Ж-жен-скій.	Какъ записанный приходятся главѣ хозяйства и главѣ своей семьи?	Сколько минуло лѣтъ или мѣсяцевъ отъ роду?	Холостъ, женатъ, вдовъ или разведенъ.	Сословіе, состояніе или званіе.	ЗДѢСЬ-ли родился, а если не здѣсь, то гдѣ именно? (Губернія, уѣздъ, городъ)	ЗДѢСЬ-ли приписъ а если не здѣсь, то именно? (для лицъ, обязанъ приписью)
1 **2** Surname, name father's name Note if the person is blind, mute, deaf-mute, deaf or imbecile	Male/Female	Relationship to the head of the family	Age	Marital status	Estate	Where was born	Where belongs

9	10	11	12	13		14	
Гдѣ обыкновенно проживаетъ: здѣсь-ли, и если не здѣсь, то гдѣ именно? (Губ.,уѣздъ, городъ).	Отмѣтка объ отсутствіи, отлучкѣ и о временномъ здѣсь пребыва-ніи.	Вѣроиспо-вѣданіе.	Родной языкъ.	Грамотность.		Занятіе, ремесло, промыселъ, должность или служба.	
				а. Умѣеть-ли читать?	б. Гдѣ обучается, обучался или кончилъ курсъ образованія?	Главное, то есть то, которое доставляетъ главныя средства для существованія.	1. Побочное или вспомогательное. 2. Положеніе по воинской повинности.
Where lives	Note about absence or temporary being	Religion	Mother tongue	Literacy If can read	Where studied	Occupation Business post a Main occupation which gives means of subsistence	Trade service 2 b 1. Secondary occupation 2. Attitude to the military service

The **1935 census** which has survived completely gives a great deal of information on the population of Latvia prior to World War 2. The **census of 1941** did not include Jews apart from Liepāja and Grobina.

Another important source is **Family Lists** as they listed the whole family together with the men on the left and women on the right as in the Revision Lists. They were mainly for statistical calculations. Family Lists for Bauske and Rēzekne are in the Latvia Database. Additions will be added as they are acquired.

Inhabitants Lists for Riga 1885/1886 are in the Latvia Database. They give information on families that may legally belong to another place. Similar to these inhabitant lists are the lists of **people residing in Courland** but belonging to other communities. These lists contain information on the families that came from Lithuania to Courland. They give information on how long the family lived in a particular town in Courland, where they came from, occupation of the head of the family and his economic situation. In many cases it is the only source of information on the family.

Passports – there are many misconceptions as regards passports.

Passport Registration Passports were not really used for travel abroad to any great extent until after the 1920s and so many of our ancestors left Lithuania or Latvia without any passport. They did require **Travel Documents** to move around the Russian Empire and these were passports for internal use. When they arrived in the place they were visiting they had to deposit the passport with the Police and this had to be renewed varying from every 3 months to every 6 months or yearly. We have no idea what determined the time interval for each registration. **Registration Books** have survived for 1876 - 1915. The most complete books are for 1900-1915. What has made this particular data of importance is that it gives places of origin. Many of the registrants were living in Lithuania reinforcing the fact that there was great movement between Latvia and Lithuania. They are not in alphabetic order so once again take a long time to work through.

Passport issuing books exist for Riga, Liepāja, Talsi, Tukums, Ludza, Aizpute and Rēzekne. These books with data in the passports as we know them for travel abroad contain information on the maiden name of the women and also minor children born after 1905. The archive has **Passport application books** for 1920-1928 and for Liepāja up to 1939 which is not complete.

Passports There are in the Archives about 700.000 passports of Jews from all over Latvia who lived in Riga in 1919-1940. Early passports from 1919-1926 contain more information than later passports 1927-1939. If there is a reference that indicates that Latvian citizenship was obtained then naturalisation files are consulted.

House Registers The Archives have registers for Riga from the end of the 19th century. The ones that have survived reasonably well are for 1919-1940. They are important because they may indicate that a family was moved to the Ghetto in 1941, deported or fled to Russia. If one compares the data with the data from the Extraordinary Commission one can get some idea of the fate of the Jews in 1941-1944. There are also registers for Liepāja, Daugavpils, Jelgava, Bauska, and Sabile and Ventspils.

The Work of the Archivists
Latvian researchers are very lucky to have dedicated archivists researching their family history. The data is held in very old files and some of the print is faded and difficult to read. Their familiarity with Jewish names and families enables them to make connections that would be impossible in less able hands. A great deal of work has been done in the past few years to computerise data and this is an ongoing project that will ensure the survival of the records. They will supply documents with translations where requested and even construct a family tree when they have been given a lot of information and consequently found many connections.

31

Jewish Firms Riga 1891	Name of the owner	Address
T.Abelmann, Timber trade	Tobias Abelmann	Pauluccistr.7
Arnoldt & Marcuse Drapery trade	Peysak (Paul) Marcuse	Gr.Sünderstr. 20
B.M.Aronsohn Agent	Behr Meyer Aronsohn	Bischofstr. 5
Bernhard Aronsohn Drapery trade	Bernhard Aronsohn	Herrenstr. 26
Jossif Markowitsch Gold Tobacco, fancy-goods	Jossif Markowitsch	Kalkstr. 5
S.Atlas Matting trade	Schmerl Atlas	Reeperstr. 4
S.Babin Old clothes trade	Selmann Babin	Marienstr. 50
Jacob Baumgart Fancy-goods trade	Jankel Baumgart	Dorpaterstr. 25
Jacob Belinki Fancy-goods trade	Jacob Belinki	Turgenjewstr. 11
Abram Bereliow Clothes, gold and silver trade	Abram Jossel Bereliow	Königstr. 1
B.Bergmann Fancy-goods trade	Benjamin Bergmann	Dünamarkt 139
Abel Berner Leather trade	Abel Berner	Gertrudstr. 81
Joseph Berner Leather and colonial goods trade	Joseph Berner	Dünamarkt 150
Bernheim & Co Hatter	Gabriel Jossel Bernheim	Elisabethstr. 10
L.Blankenstein Clothes trade	Leib son of Berel Blankenstein	Kalkstr. 36

S.A.Blechmann & Söhne Fashion goods trade	Samuel Abraham Blechmann and sons Abraham and Lewin	Sünderstr. 9
A.Blum Small trade	Abel Blum	Herrenstr. 24
B.Blumberg Oats trade	Benjamin Blumberg	Steinstr. 22
Moses Blumenfeld Old clothes trade	Moses Blumenfeld	Königstr. 24
A.Blumenthal Calf skin trade	Aron Blumenthal, Hulda Blumenthal	Weberstr. 11
Moritz Blumenthal Pelts trade	Moses (Moritz) Blumenthal, Theophile Blumenthal	Theater-Boulv. 6
N.Blumethal Agricultural goods trade	Nechemja Heimann Blumenthal, Jacob, Julius, Philipp and Jeannot Blumenthal	Weberstr 18 and Herrenstr. 25
Mendel Blumes Glas and faience-goods trade	Mendel son of Berel Blumes	Königstr. 16
S.Brakmann Colonial goods trade	Selig son of Daniel Brakmann	Kalkstr. 17
Moses Braun Sohn Sugar & Kerosene	Sara née Winzburg, Judel Braun	Münzstr. 16
Feitel Cahn Felt trade	Feitel Cahn	Gertrudstr. 105
M.Cahn Clock, gold and silver trade	Moissei Cahn	Herrenstr. 1
M.A.Cahn Leather trade	Mendel Cahn	Gr.Mosk.Str. 70
Michel Schmerl Cahn Fur trade	Michel son of Schmerl Cahn	Münzstr. 14

J.David Chait Small trade	Itzig David Chait	Dünamarkt 153
Georg Danziger Fashion goods trade	Hosias Georg Danziger	Kalkstr. 15
Herm. Danziger Writing materials trade	Hermann Danziger	Sünderstr. 6
Louis Edelberg Gold and silver trade	Louis Edelberg	Alexanderstr. 5
S.M.Eliasberg Timber trade	Issay son of Moisey Eliasberg, Samuel Eliasberg	Wallstr. 30
A.Eliasstamm Agricultural goods trade	Adolph Graumann Eliasstamm	Marstallstr. 17
B.Elkan Leather	Benjamin Elkan	Schaalstr. 7
Chr.Ellermann Granite stone trade	Victor Idelsohn	Gr.Mosk.Str. 22
Sch.Engelsohn Tobacco trade	Schmul son of Leib Engelsohn	Gr.Sünderstr. 13
Moses A.Epstein Silver table-ware trade	Simon son of Abram Epstein	Kl.Münzstr. 3
S.O.Epstein Cheese and butter trade	Schmul son of Oscher Epstein	Scharrenstr. 4
D.Essiedt Tobacco, salt, colonial goods trade	David Essiedt, Jacob Essiedt	Dorpaterstr. 4
Louis Feitelberg Small and drapery trade	Lewin Feitelberg	Herrenstr. 21
Moritz Feitelberg Fashion goods trade	Moritz Feitelberg, Mahra Feitelberg	Gr.Sünderstr. 6
H.Feitelsohn Drapery trade	Hermann Feitelsohn	Weberstr. 3

34

L.Fellmann Corn trade	Leib Jankel Fellmann	Mühlenstr. 126
David Friedenberg Inn-keeper	David Friedenberg	Mühlenstr. 96
I.Friedmann & Co Sugar trade	Isidor Moritz Friedmann	Kaufstr. 21
S.Fromhold Shoe trade	Selig Fromhold	Kaufstr. 24
U.M.Frumkin Corn trade	Ure son of Meier Frumkin	Gr.Königstr. 29
H.Gold and I.Grün Fashion goods trade	Hirsch Gold and Israel Grün	Gr.Sünderstr. 20
Hirsch Gordon Leather trade	Hirsch Gordon	Gr.Mosk. Str. 83
Jacob Gottlieb Clothes trade	Jankel son of Wulf Gottlieb	Kalkstr. 10
Jean Gottlieb Drapery and fashion goods trade	Jean Gottlieb	Alexanderstr. 9
M.Grünblatt Drapery trade	Martin son of Raphael Grünblatt	Sünderstr. 14
Wulf Grüntuch Drapery trade	Wulf Grüntuch	Gr.Mosk.Str. 105
Guttschewsky & Jürgensohn Lavatory cleaning	Joseph Kalmann Berkowitz; Alex. Friedrich Jürgensohn	Thurmstr. 25
D.Hahn Inn keeper	David Hahn	Kl.Neustr. 1
E.Hellmann Drapery	Emil Hellmann	Herrenstr. 14
Hellmann & Nieburg Drapery Trade	Nathan Nieburg, Jette Nieburg nee Kramm	Scheunenstr. 13
B.Henfenstein Timber trade	Berka Henfenstein	Gr.Mosk Str. 44
J.Herrmann Inn keeper	Julius Herrmann	Kramerstr. 4

Herzenberg & Meyerowitz Drapery trade	Louis Herzenberg, Moritz Meyerowitz	Gr.Sünderstr. 25
Moritz Herzfeld Corn trade	Moritz Herzfeld	Pauluccistr. 8
J.Herzmark Glass goods trade	Jossel Herzmark	Gr.Sünderstr. 5
H.A.Hirschberg Fancy and small goods trade	Rosalia Hirschberg, nee Königsfest	Gr.Sünderstr. 27
Kalmann Hirschhorn Buying and selling of different goods	Kalmann Hirschhorn	Marienstr. 17
St.Petersburger Fensterglasmagazin A.N.Hodes Glass goods trade	Abram Nochum son of Berel Hodes	Herrenstr. 28
Lewin O.Hoffmann Pelts trade	Lewin Hoffmann	Mühlenstr. 122
J.Holländer Clothes trade	Joseph Holländer	Kalkstr. 31
M.Hotz Steel goods trade	Mowscha Hotz	Sünderstr. 18
L.M.Hurewitz Corn, butter, honey, oil trade	Leibe son of Mowscha Hurewitz	Elisabethstr. 95
Moses J.Hurewitsch Not stated	Moses Itzig Hurewitsch	Parkstr. 6
David Jappa Fur trade	David Jappa	Sünderstr. 7
Sima M.Jefet Tobacco trade	Sima son of Moisey Jefet	Alexanderstr. 28
H.I.Immermann Fashion and fancy goods trade, dressmaker	Fanny Immermann	Kalkstr. 15a

36

Hillel Joffe Leather trade	Hillel Joffe	Kl.Sünderstr. 3
Leopold Isermann Agricultural goods trade	Leopold Isermann	Dorpaterstr. 20
Lipmann Itziksohn Glass, soup, herring trade	Lipmann son of Itzik Itziksoh	Herrenstr. 30
Eduard Judelowitz Leather trade	Eduard Judelowitz	Kämmereistr. 5/7
Aron Kahn drapery	Aron Kahn	Herrenstr. 23
Simon Kahn Corn trade	Simon Kahn	Weberstr. 9
Schmul Kahn Fashion and drapery trade	Schmul Kahn	Alexanderstr. 114
L.Kamenetzky Sawmill	Lipe son of Jankel Kamenetzky	Pielenhofsche Str. 1
N.Kaschdan Uniform goods trade	Nissen Itzig son of Aron Kaschdan	Kalkstr.6
P.S.Kanter Ironmongery trade	Pinkus son of Schlom Kanter	Steinstr. 8
Leibe Kaplun Fashion goods trade	Leibe son of Kaimak Kaplun, Schimen Behrmann	Dorpater Str. 7
M.Kassel Drapery trade	Mensel Kassel	Lagestr. 1
N.Kirsner Corn trade	Nachmann Kirsner	Reeperstr. 5
S.Kirstein Coffin trade	Simon Kirstein	Petrikirchenstr. 25
Nachmann Klink Gold and silver trade	Nachmann Klink	Herrenstr. 24
N.Knopping Small trade Pedlar	Nachmann Hirsch Knopping, Julius Kahn	Herrenstr. 1

Israel Kramer	Israel Kramer	Gr.Str. 93
S.Kramer	Salomon Moses	
Drapery trade	Grünfeldt called	Gr.Str. 110
	Kramer	
M.Kron Fashion	Meyer Kron	Sünderstr. 25
Adolf Levy	Adolf (Abram Elkan)	Kaufstr. 10
Writing goods trade	Levy	
Max Levy	Max Levy	Schmiedestr. 44
Corn export		
I.Levy	Srol (Israel) son of	Marienstr. 13
Clothes trade	Itzik Levy	
Leon Lew		Herrenstr. 4
	Leon Lew	
Bank and exchange		
Leibe Itzikowitsch		Neustr. 27
Lewin	Leibe son of Itzik	
Herring and salt trade	Lewin	
Gebrüder Lewstein	Israel Lewstein,	Sadownikowstr.
Corn export-import	Salomon Lewstein	9
Salman Lewstein	Salomon Lewstein	
Colonial goods,		Alexanderstr. 88
firewood trade		
G.Liebesmann	Gutmann	
Men's clothes, fancy	Liebesmann	Alexanderb. 11
trade		
Noach Lifschitz &	Leib Lifschitz,	
Sohn	Samuel David	Sünderstr. 2
Tobacco trade	Lifschitz	
M.Löwenstamm	Marcus	
Coffee, sugar and	Löwenstamm	Sünderstr. 2
tea trade		
J.Loewenstein	Jacob Loewenstein	Scheunenstr. 18
Toys trade		
J.Lozky	Jankel son of Itzik	Steinstr. 3
Flour trade	Lozky	
W.Luntz	Wulf son of Jankel	Schmiedestr. 66
Rent of korobka tax	Luntz	
Kosher meat tax		

Ludwig Lurie Small trade	Ludwig Lurie	Sünderstr. 3
Moritz Machmonnik Clothes trade	Mowscha (Moritz) Machmonnik	Wallstr. 20
A.S.Maikapar Tobacco factory and trade	Abram Samuil Maikapar	Kalkstr. Haus d. Ulei
Mattisohn & Sack Leather trade	Srol Aron Mattisohn, Samuel (Jannot) son of Israel Sack	Sünderstr. 34
S.Meisel & Söhne Iron and aniline dye trade	Moritz Meisel	Herrenstr. 20
M.Micheless Firewood trade	Moses son of Lew Micheless	Bischofstr. 5
Max Michelsohn Agent	Mordechay (Max) Michelsohn	Gr. Königstr. 32
M.Minz contracts	Michel Minz	Thronfolgerboul. 33
Abram Moschkin Drinks trade	Abram Moschkin	Romanowstr. 127
Wulf Mowschensohn Corn trade	Wulf Mowschensohn	Suworowstr. 6
Markus Mulner Clothes and linen trade	Markus Mulner	Dünamarkt 144/145
J.Ch.Muschat Drapery trade	Jossel son of Chaim Muschat	Suworowstr. 15
Nathansohn & Bernheim Fancy and fashion goods trade	Jankel Mowscha Nathansohn, Sarah Nathansohn	Gr.Sünderstr. 17
I.Neuberg Drapery trade	Israel Neuberg	Kalkstr. 15

S.H.Neumark Drapery trade	Salman son of Hirsch Neumark	Gr.Mosk. Str. 59
Sch.Nimzowitsch Firewood trade	Schaje son of abram Nimzowitsch	Münstereistr. 6
W.Nogaler Linen trade	Wulf Boruch Nogaler	Kaufstr. 14
Nochim Rabinowitsch Firewood trade	Nochim so of Jankel Rabinowitsch	Gr.Mosk. Str. 21
J.L.Rappoport Firewood trade	Jeruchim Leibe Rappoport	Dünaufer Str. 53
Mowscha Rappoport Firewood trade	Kreine Elka Rappoport	Smolensker Str. 12
P.Ch.Rattner Herring and salt trade	Peisack son of Chaim Rattner	Poststr. 5
H.Rendel Drapery and fashion goods trade	Hirsch Rendel	Gr.Str. 95
M.Rosenfeld Corn trade	Mowscha Rosenfeld	Dünauferstr. 7
Itzik Rosenfeld Furniture trade	Itzik son of Chatzkel Rosenfeld	Theaterboul. 10
J.Rottermundt Inn keeper	Julius David Rottermundt	Scheunenstr. 19
Hanne Rubin Clothes, gold and silver trade	Hanne Rubin neé Goldzicker	Pferdestr. 12
Feige Rubin Hotel keeper	Feige Rubin	Gr.Königsstr. 45
M.Rukeyser & Söhne Drapery trade	Isidor Rukeyser, Hermann Rukeyser	Gr.Mümzstr. 6
R.Salgaller Ironmongery trade	Ruben Naftali Salgaller	Kurmanowstr. 21a

J.Salomonsohn Drapery trade	Itzig Moses Salomonsohn	Rathauspl. 1
L.S.Salomonsohn Leather Fur	Laser Salomon Salomonsohn	Newastr. 12
Heymann Salzmann Pedlar	Heymann Salzmann	Gr.Sünderstr. 10/12
E.Schaitan Tobacco and fancy trade	Jefet Schalom son of Ilja Schaitan	Kalkstr. 6
L.Schalit Firewood trade	Leib son of Morduch Schalit	Gr.Königstr. 16
Schlom Schalit Firewood trade	Schlom Schalit	Smolensker Str. 2
J.Schapiro Agricultural goods trade	Jossel (Joseph) Schapiro	Jesuskirchenstr. 8
Nochum Leibowitsch Schapiro Firewood trade	Nochum son of Leib Schapiro	Elisabethstr. 95
S.Schapiro Leather and dye trade	Schmul Schapiro	Schwimmstr. 13
Alex. L. Schaskolsky Secondhand goods shop	Alexander sonLasar Schaskolsky,Sophie (Sore) daughter of Lasar Aronsohn, nee Schaskolsky	Gr.Sünderstr.18
David Schereschewsky Steel Goods	David Schereschewsky	Gr.Mosk.Str. 105
Mendel Schereschewsky Wool trade	Mendel son of Hessel Schereschewsky	Kl.Neustr. 5
S.Schereschewsky Steel and iron goods trade	Schmul son of Berel Schereschewsky	Kl.Neustr. 4

41

Jossel Schermann Corn and flour trade	Jossesl Schermann	Wendensche Str. 1
Gebr. Schlamowitz Not stated	Wulf Schlamowitz, Salkins Moses Schlamowitz	Kaufstr. 16
Boruch Schlapobersky Matting trade	Boruch Schlapobersky	Eliasstr. 13
G.Schönfeldt Steel goods trade	Gerson Schönfeldt, Abram Blumberg	Gr:Sünderstr. 12/14
D.Schwarzbort Sugar trade	David son of Mowscha Schwarzbort	Gr.Schmiedestr. 66
Jankel Silbermann Corn trade	Jankel Silbermann	Marienstr. 110
L.Silpert Fire and building wood trade	Liebermann son of Leiser Silpert	Dünauferstr. 8/9
Max Simsohn Fashion goods trade	Max Simsohn	Herrenstr. 25
J.Slutzkin Leather trade	Juda Itzka Slutzkin	Schwimmstr. 24
A.Switgall Clothes trade	Abraham son of Schiman Switgall	Kalkstr. 13
S.M.Switgall Clothes trade	Mowscha Switgall	Kl.Königstr. 17
Tawel Tawjew Leather trade	Chwole Tawjew	Kurmanowstr. 15
L.Thal Fashion goods trade	Lipmann Thal	Kalkstr. 9
D.Trambatzky Meat trade	David Trambatzky	Scharrenstr. 8
Moses Trubek Drapery trade	Mowscha (Moses) Trubek	Wacholderstr. 4
E.Weinberg Drapery trade	Elias Itzik Weinberg	Dorpaterstr. 7
Manne Weinberg Small trade	Manne Weinberg	Gr.Sünderstr. 3

B.Weinreich Drapery trade	Benjamin Weinreich	Gr.Mosk.Str. 91
Chaim Weissager Gold and silver trade	Chaim Weissager	Herrenstr. 5
W.Weissager Gold and silver trade	Wulff Weissager	Kalkstr. 10
J.Werth Corn trade	Itzik Lewin Werth	Schwimmstr. 16
Sch. Werth Drapery	Schaie Lewin Werth	Gr.Mosk. Str. 77
L.Wilenkin Tea trade	Laser Wilenkin	Gr.Jungferstr. 11
S.A.Wolf Corn trade	Sender Abaram Wolf	Elisabethstr. 101
Jacob Wolpert Old clothes and drapery trade	Jacob Wolpert	Gr:Mosk Str. 11
M.Wulfsohn & Sohn Hat and bonnet trade	Moses Wulfsohn, Schmul Leib Wulfsohn	Dünamarkt 75/76
L.Zinnemann Drapery trade	Chaim Leibe Zinnemann	Rathausplatz 1

Other Archives in Latvia

Depending on the shtetl you are researching in Latvia, you may have other archives to contact.

Vital records from 1906 are held in the Latvian Archives of the Registry Department of the Ministry of Justice in Riga. Although the State Historical Archives indicates that the holdings of the Registry Department range only up to 1921, documents from as late as 1930 have been obtained and it appears that death records exist up to 1944.

This archive apparently does not have the facilities to accept foreign currency, so it bills through the Latvian Embassy of your Country.

The embassy will send a notification that documents have been received, and will request payment by money order. The embassy will then mail the documents, which are actually certified abstracts. The abstracts are entirely in Latvian, and are not translated. A fee is charged even if documents are not found; a certificate to that effect will be issued, along with a statement of which records were searched in vain. [6]

The address of the Registry Office in Riga is:
Archives of the Registry Dept,
Kalku Street 24,
LV-1050, Riga
Latvia

Vital Records from 1921 are in offices in the following districts:
Aizkraukle, Alūksne, Balvi, Bauska, Cēsis, Daugavpils, Dobele, Gulbene, Jekabpils, Jelgava, Krāslava, Kuldīga, Liepāja, Limbazi, Ludza, Madona, Ogre, Preili, Rēzekne, Riga, Saldus, Talsi, Tukums, Valka, Valmiera and Ventspils.

It is worthwhile applying to the Kalku Street Office about documents from 1921 before applying to these regional district offices because The Registry Office has been known to supply some documents dating as late as 1940. Researchers who have experience in dealing with the Kalku Street Archive are requested to send the information to Latvia SIG.

Vitebsk
After the Third Partition of Poland in 1795 Latgale became part of Vitebsk Province (Vitebsk gubernia) in the Russian Empire. Major shtetlach of Latgale that were in Vitebsk are Daugavpils (Dvinsk), Krāslava, Dagda, Rēzekne (Rēzhitze), Ludza (Lutsin) and Preili. Records for these shtetlach may be found in the Latvian State Historical Archives or in Minsk in the National Historical Archives of Belarus.

Vitebsk was the largest town in Vitebsk gubernia and a major cultural centre. It was the home of the famous artists Yehuda Pen and Marc Chagall as well as many others. In 1919 Vitebsk gubernia was divided up and Latgale once again became part of Latvia.

Part of Vitebsk was included in Belarus illustrating once again how changing borders can affect the location of documents in Archives.

Research in the former Russian Empire [9]

You should always extend the boundaries of your search, as our ancestors were migrants. If archives are unable to find details of your family you should consider that a great number of Latvians came from Lithuania and Belarus.

Lithuania

An excellent resource on Lithuania is the Litvak SIG Web site: <http://www.Jewishgen.org/litvak>.
A new booklet has been published by JGSGB entitled-
A Guide to Jewish Genealogy in Lithuania, by Sam Aaron
ISBN: 0 9537669 8 5

The Lithuanian State Historical Archives in Vilnius have vital records and some revision lists.
    Lietuvos Valstybes Istorijos Archyvas (LVIA)
    Gerosios 10, Vilnius, Lithuania
    LT-03134
    Director: Ms Laima Trasvaiste
    Chief Archivist: Ms Galina Baranova

The Kaunas State Archives do not have vital records but have other records such as military, legal and tax records, as well as revision lists for cities and towns of the former Kovno gubernia.
    Kauno Apygardos Archyvas
    Maironio 28a LT-44249, Kaunas
    Chief Archivist: Ms Vitalija Gircyte

Belarus

The Belarus SIG website at <http://www.Jewishgen.org/belarus> is constantly expanding, and is an excellent source of information on the region covered by present-day Belarus.

    The name Belarus only appeared after the Russian Revolution in 1919. The region had belonged to many different countries at different times and this complicated the location of records. Jews arrived in Grodno and Brest in the late 1380s from Poland and Germany. There were more than 60,000 Jews prior to the 1770s and 1,250 000 prior to the World War I. [7]

Jews were registered in different communities. Records for Minsk are in the National Historical Archives and those of Grodno in the Central Historical Archives. After Vitebsk Province was split up, part of it went to the Latgale region of Latvia, part to Belarus, part to Poland and part to Lithuania.

The districts of Daugavpils, Ludza and Rézekne in the modern Latgale area of Latvia were in Vitebsk Province before 1917 and therefore the records may be in the Minsk Archives:
National Historical Archives of Belarus
Krapotkina Street 55, Minsk, Belarus

Some lists that are in this Archive are:
revision lists for Rēzekne and Ludza for 1811
1850 lists of citizens and merchants of Ludza
lists of Jews of Vitebsk Province living in rural areas 1889
1874 census of Rēzekne and Varaklani
1874 census of Daugavpils
1874 census of Dagda
1874 census of Polotsk (partial)
1874 list of home owners of Gostini (Glazmanka) [8]

Records for the former Grodno gubernia are housed in the Minsk Archive:
Central State Historical Archive of the Belarus SSR (MINSK)
220038, Minsk, ul. Kozlova, 26.

The Family History Library has filmed a great number of Jewish records in Minsk.

Latvia, as part of the Russian Empire, was subject to its passport and travel document laws.

Passports, travel documents and residence permits

Residence permits could be issued only in the place of permanent residence, and for Jews were issued only in the Pale of Settlement. Permits were only valid in places in the Pale where Jews were permitted to live, temporarily or permanently. They also received documents (billets) which stated how long they could be away from the Pale, which were added to the residence permit.

If Jews left the Pale of Settlement they had to show the police both residence permit and document, which confirmed their right to live in or out of the Pale. If the absence was for not more than six months, and in the same district or in another not further than 50 verst (3500 feet or 1.06 km) away, then no document was required.

There were also **passport books** (*pasportnaya knizhka*), and **passports** of one sheet in white, yellow or blue. The reason for the different colours is not clear, but may have been connected to military service. Petty bourgeois, craftsmen and countrymen received passport books, which were issued for five years. If the person changed communities the passport was replaced. The person had to pay the annual fee for the passport book by the 31 December, or the passport could be forfeited until full payment was made.

Passports of one sheet were issued for not more than a year. They contained surname, given name, father's name, occupation, age, religion, place of residence, class (estate), distinctive marks, destination, duration of and reason for travel.

A passport for travelling abroad was issued by the head of the province or general governor. A governor was head of one province (e.g.Governor of Courland province). A general governor was head of many provinces (e.g. a Baltic General Governor of Courland, Livland and Estland).

Applicants had to write a request to the governor or general governor, showing a certificate from the police to say that there were no obstacles to going abroad, or a guarantee from reliable people. Jewish applicants had to have paid all taxes, have no debts and not be eligible for military service. They needed permission from the Elected Elders (the Kahal) to leave the community. Some young people who received permission to go abroad for study never returned.

Merchants who went abroad to resolve commercial problems received passports for a year. Russian citizens could stay abroad for five years. Registers for exit permits were kept for each year. These stated the name of the community whence the holders came, and were housed in the State Archives or the governor's office.

The "rules about passports" were promulgated in the Russian Empire in 1903 but they were based on many previous laws which were in force at the beginning of the 19th century.

Prof Edward Anders sponsored a project to obtain passport photographs for inhabitants of Libau. I have summarised the paper written by Senior Archivist Irina Veinberga who headed the project.

The archival documents used in this project provide a source for all interested individuals, enabling them to update information on individual persons and the whole Jewish community of Liepāja during the period of the Latvian republic 1918-1940.

The passport issuance books are a component of the fond (group of stored records) of the Liepāja Prefecture which was authorized under the law of 1919 to distribute the passports of Latvian citizens. Under the law, from May 4, 1921 all citizens of Jewish nationality who had residence permits in the Russian empire, received the right to obtain passports as Latvian citizens. Thus, according to the legislation of the Latvian republic, all persons who had reached the age of 16 years received a passport. This meant that information on these persons was stored in the appropriate documents and, in particular, documents of the prefecture, which had issued the passport.

Unfortunately no complete set of passport books exists in the fond of the Liepāja Prefecture. The documents on the "first" Latvian passports are fragmentary; there are only 2 books -1921 and May - August of 1927. Passports that were issued in Liepāja from August 18, 1927 until the last issued on September 18, 1940 have fortunately survived in a better condition and there are 63,020 passports. All books from August 18 1927 until September 18 1940 are numbered and this gives an indirect indication of the number of Liepāja adult inhabitants.

Series and numbers of the passport This important information can be used for cross analysis with other documents, in particular, house registers.

Passport Date is used as an aid to research when only the age and residence of the person in a certain period is known.
As passports were issued on attaining 16 years of age it is possible to find a record of the passport.

Surname and name This will be the official fixed spelling which appears as a rule in all other documents given after issue of the passport. In the passports "of the new sample", since 1927 the patronymic was not specified.

Birth date and birth place The inclusion of this information in the passport allows a connection with other documents such as vital records, enabling additional information to be obtained about parents and the establishment of their relationship.

Marital status This very important information, especially for women, allows us in combination with other data to identify individuals.

Children up to age 16 years Under the law, passports of children under 16 years of age were listed in the passport of the mother, with the name of the child and date of birth. When the child received a passport on reaching the designated age or in certain other cases that were specified by the law, a special column was filled out with a mark indicating that a personal passport was distributed to the child. Since this also records the date of distribution and its series and number, it permits one to continue the search for information and allows accurate interpretation of the record.

The passport of a married woman is based on the passport of the husband, with his passport number and date of issue, certificate of rabbi who presided at the marriage and details of date and place of event etc. A mark in the passport about change of marital status signifies that there is information on divorce and refers one to the number and date of the document of the appropriate judicial authority which has accepted the decision. The law on the issuance of passports prescribed that if a woman did not keep the surname of her husband after marriage or divorce, then she should receive a new passport one month later.

Notation about payment of a State Tax or about exemption from its payment The information in this column, gives an idea of the financial situation of the family and in particular about the reason they were exempted from the payment which was 1 lat.

Annulment of the passport This very important information is about changing a surname because of marriage with a foreigner which was a reason to change citizenship and indicates a loss of the Latvian one. At the same time it gives indirect information about emigration or change of the place of residence. If the passport was annulled because of death of the person one finds here an accurate date of death. It is especially important when it specifies that death occurred during the Holocaust because in some cases the exact date is stated.

Photographs There is a very special place in these documents for the photos of the owners of the passports. They are of excellent quality and superbly kept. They give incomparable emotional colouring to the documents. Having photographs is rare and the researcher receives not only documentary information on the individual person, but also a real image of the person who is being researched. "Wonderful, spiritual faces"…are seen. Sometimes photos are absent, but there is always a mark to indicate that this is because of illness or advanced age, or because the material was not up to standard. A very small number of photos were lost. 142 of 10116 photographs are not available. Thus at the disposal of the archive there are at present about 10,000 photos. There are also photos of the majority of victims of the Holocaust (among the adult population).

The signature The presence of a signature helps in some cases to specify the spelling of a surname, or, on occasion if there are losses of parts of the document then a signed name helps establish a surname of the owner of the passport. Where a signature is absent as is the case with illiteracy of the owner of the passport then a special mark was made.

Fingerprint The print of an index finger of the right hand of the owner of the passport was an obligatory element for such documents as passports, passport books etc. In certain cases it may serve as one of the most important elements of identification of the person where the documents contain contradictory information.

Similar documents were kept for other places of Latvia. Their degree of preservation and whether they are complete is varied.

There is an ongoing debate as to whether Jews needed passports when they left Latvia. The following is a personal communication received from Nicholas J. Evans.

Whilst the migrants crossing the border with Germany or Austria could do so illegally - without the necessary paperwork - those leaving via the Baltic ports had to be in possession of an official passport before embarkation could occur. Such documentation could be costly and time-consuming to obtain. However, as officials investigating the mass emigration of Russians regularly noted in their correspondence it was possible to obtain documentation upon arrival at the port of embarkation 'for a fee'. Gendarmes (police) were stationed at the Libau quayside 24 hours before embarkation took place and made certain that everyone leaving had some form of documentation. Whether or not the people listed on a passport were related was seemingly irrelevant. Crucially it would have been impossible for the officials issuing the passports to know whether or not an individual was legally permitted to leave. Demand was so great that the passport office for Courland relocated from the capital Mitau to the port of Libau.

Please see page 30 and 46 for further details on passports.

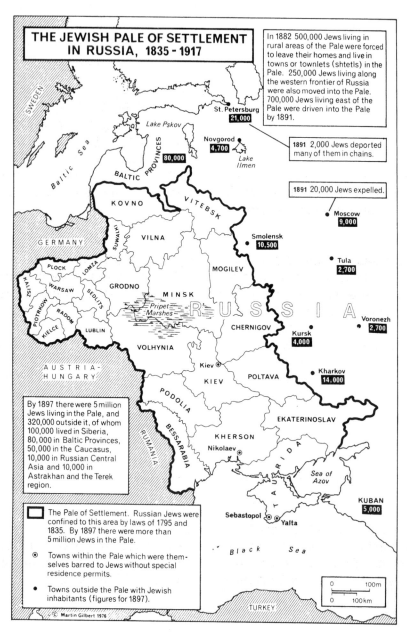

THE JEWISH PALE OF SETTLEMENT IN RUSSIA, 1835 - 1917

In 1882 500,000 Jews living in rural areas of the Pale were forced to leave their homes and live in towns or townlets (shtetls) in the Pale. 250,000 Jews living along the western frontier of Russia were also moved into the Pale. 700,000 Jews living east of the Pale were driven into the Pale by 1891.

1891 2,000 Jews deported many of them in chains.

1891 20,000 Jews expelled.

SWEDEN

Baltic Sea

Lake Pskov

St. Petersburg **21,000**

Novgorod **4,700**
Lake Ilmen

80,000

BALTIC PROVINCES

KOVNO

VITEBSK

GERMANY

SUWALKI

VILNA

Smolensk **10,500**

Moscow **9,000**

PLOCK

LOMZA

MOGILEV

Tula **2,700**

KALISZ

WARSAW

SEDLITS

GRODNO

MINSK

Pripet Marshes

R U S S I A

PIOTRKOW

RADOM

LUBLIN

CHERNIGOV

Voronezh **2,700**

KIELCE

VOLHYNIA

Kursk **4,000**

AUSTRIA-HUNGARY

Kiev

KIEV

POLTAVA

Kharkov **14,000**

PODOLIA

By 1897 there were 5 million Jews living in the Pale, and 320,000 outside it, of whom 100,000 lived in Siberia, 80,000 in Baltic Provinces, 50,000 in the Caucasus, 10,000 in Russian Central Asia and 10,000 in Astrakhan and the Terek region.

BESSARABIA

RUMANIA

EKATERINOSLAV

KHERSON

Nikolaev

TAURIDA

Sea of Azov

KUBAN **5,000**

The Pale of Settlement. Russian Jews were confined to this area by laws of 1795 and 1835. By 1897 there were more than 5 million Jews in the Pale.

Sebastopol
Yalta

Towns within the Pale which were themselves barred to Jews without special residence permits.

B l a c k   S e a

Towns outside the Pale with Jewish inhabitants (figures for 1897).

0   100m
0   100km

© Martin Gilbert 1976

TURKEY

The Routledge Atlas of Jewish History by Martin Gilbert Reprinted 1995 Published with permission from Routledge Publishers.

52

Legal records can be helpful. Jews were in danger of breaking the law, since there were more than 650 restrictions with which they had to comply. District level court records are in Minsk and Grodno archives.

The first Russian population census, known as the **Revision Lists** (**reviskaya skazka**), was started in 1719, but not finished until about 1727. It served a dual purpose: military conscription, which had been introduced in 1699, and personal taxation. So many citizens tried to avoid being counted that the authorities were forced to employ soldiers to enforce the law. Despite torture, executions and heavy fines, evasion was widespread.

In the second half of the 19th century there were local censuses of householders which were taken from time to time in various areas; these are a major source of genealogical information. Records were kept of unprivileged townsmen, petty bourgeois merchants, craftsmen and workers, as well as of rural peasant farmers. These lists of taxpayers were compiled every 10-20 years between 1719 and 1858 in each town, district or rural area. Jews did not appear on the revision lists until after the third partition of Poland in 1795 when they became Russian subjects.

Gubernski vedomosti[10] were official Government newspapers published in all parts of the Russian Empire in each region. They began in 1838 in Bialystock, Ekaterinoslav, Grodno, Minsk and Vitebsk, to name but a few. Publication in Courland started in 1852 and in Livland in 1853. The information is varied, but one may find names of soldiers, lists of wanted persons often with physical descriptions, trade and private announcements and lists of missing persons. Publications are in German only for 1853, German and Russian for 1866-1885 and Russian only from 1886-1915.

Emigration[11]

The pogroms of 1881 in Russia, exacerbated by rapid population increase and economic conditions, encouraged far greater numbers of Jews to leave Russia. In the 1890s and early 1900s more Jews began to leave the Pale as intense commercial rivalry between British and German steamship operators forced down the price of passage across the Atlantic. Our ancestors generally left by making the overland trek to the ports of Antwerp, Bremen, Hamburg, Rotterdam or Liepāja (Libau). The ships leaving Libau originated from Riga, but called into the Winter Harbour at Libau to collect ponies and emigrants.

The journey to Hull or London would have taken four or five days, but after the Kiel Canal was opened the journey time was reduced by a day as the vessels could then avoid travel via Copenhagen.

Tickets were purchased through local agents operating in the Pale for services operated by the United Steamship Shipping Company - or DFDS - and the Wilson Line of Hull. Emigrants could purchase tickets to England, South Africa or America. Passengers generally travelled indirectly via Britain, as this was cheaper than purchasing direct tickets to their eventual destination. From Hull or London they would then cross Britain by train to the places of embarkation for their final destination. Trans-Pennine rail services between the Humber ports and Liverpool were developed in 1840. Migrants arriving at Grimsby or Hull were transported via train within hours of their arrival in Britain. Helpful links to sites dealing with emigration can be found by clicking on:
<http://www.abdn.ac.uk/emigration/links.html Aberdeen University>
<http://linktoyourroots.hamburg.de>
Hamburg Passenger Lists   see page 58
<http://www.Jewishgen.org/databases/EIDB/ Ellis Island>
<http://home.att.net/%7Ewee-monster/onlinelists.html>
<http://www.theshipslist.com/>

Extract from *The Port Jews of Libau*, 1880-1914, by Nicholas J. Evans.

Little attention has been paid to the contribution of Libau (the modern day port of Liepāja) in the development of a distinctive port Jewish community in the Russian Baltic. In Libau Jewish merchants worked alongside their non-Jewish counterparts.

The Rights of the Jews in Courland within the Russian Empire

When the partition of the kingdom of Poland began in 1772, Imperial Russia found herself in control of the largest concentration of Jews in Europe. Though most lived in what became defined as the Pale of Settlement, the westward expansion of Russia meant that, by the time of Nicholas II's accession, there were sizeable Jewish communities in Russia's vibrant maritime centres at St. Petersburg, Riga, Jacobstadt and Libau. Each port lay within a different province of Imperial Russia and commercial rivalry between them was rife. Each had an active Jewish mercantile Courland community and as debate raged as to the rights to be given to Jews living in both urban and rural areas throughout Russia, so the influence that Jews exercised in maritime life was similarly questioned.

Though life in the Pale was growing increasingly intolerable, the economic strength that port Jewish commerce represented in other parts of Russia was so important that Jews who worked in Riga were granted greater freedom of mobility to trade, so that other rival ports, where they were less constrained, would not disturb the predominance of Russia's second-largest port. Even though many Jews were expelled from St. Petersburg, Riga and Libau in the early 1890s, Riga's role as the main port Jewish community in the Baltic continued to grow as one of Russia's largest ports expanded throughout the nineteenth century, helped by the rights awarded to her Jewish merchants in the mid eighteenth century.

Even though they suffered discrimination because of their faith, the Jews of Libau were still free to participate in the commerce of the land, because of their commercial acumen and because of the revenues generated through the taxes imposed upon them. Under successive Imperial Russian edicts, they faced increased threats to the rights they had enjoyed under the protection of the nobility prior to 1795. But such incursions upon their rights were often challenged, not by the Dukes of Courland, but by their noble subordinates who recognised the important contribution that Jewish merchants made to Baltic commerce, and their own revenues, as the port developed.

The Development of Libau's Port Jewish Community

The port of Libau, unlike the neighbouring ports of Riga and St. Petersburg, did not 'close' each winter when the ice closed much of the Baltic to navigation. Because of the emergence of the port as an outlet for mass migration in the early 1890s, Libau's resident Jewish population acquired importance and developed an identity independently of the role it played in the export of agrarian produce. This 'market' in the movement of humans transformed Libau into one of the world's leading centres for westward migration, providing Libau's Jewish merchants with the opportunity to profit from a trade that was 'open' to them.

Emigration grew to become an important aspect of Baltic commerce. As Libau developed throughout the 1890s and early 1900's as a centre for outward migration from Russia, so her Jews were increasingly important as facilitators of this trade. The large number of Russian and Polish Jewish emigrants leaving through the port of Libau continued to grow at an alarming rate. Only when Libau was unable to facilitate all of the Jews that desired to emigrate would 'surplus' Jewish emigrants be sent through Riga (or to a lesser extent the Finnish port of Hangö).

It was of no surprise that so many chose to emigrate via the port of Libau. The rail link that had opened between it and Romny in 1880 also linked the port with Kovno – the *gubernia* that exported more Jews to South Africa than any other region of the Pale – and other important sources of western immigrant origin. Though a passport was often required, the gendarmes policing access to the port were as open to bribery as those policing the German and Austrian land borders. The commencement of direct steamship services by the Russian American Line and the Russian Volunteer Fleet (both in 1906) between Libau and New York did not improve matters because the checks in place at Libau were far from adequate.

Conclusion

Libau was of first-rank importance as an *entrepôt* for the export of goods such as timber, grain, eggs and butter that arose because of the expansion of the transport system within and without Imperial Russia. Though Jews were forcibly moved from some of Russia's Baltic ports throughout the seventeenth, eighteenth and nineteenth centuries, the freedoms enjoyed by the Baltic-Jews of Courland continued to be allowed to Jews in Libau and Riga because their activities were so economically advantageous to an industrialising Russia.

Jews within the Pale, in Libau itself and at her harbour profited from the movement of such goods. As the need to leave Russia intensified in the wake of the Kishinev pogrom and the deterioration of life in the Pale, Danish and British shipping lines that had for decades shipped commodities such as timber, eggs and ponies (brokered by Jewish agents) began to export Jews as a staple commodity.

The availability of shipping from a port within the Russian empire enabled many Jews from Libau, the Baltic and within the Pale itself to evade the intensive medical inspections that had been introduced along the Russian border with Germany in the wake of the 1892 cholera epidemic at Hamburg. Though Libau provided a nearby port through which so many could emigrate, transmigrate or work their passage to the West, the dire state in which so many passengers were transported posed both a visible and invisible threat to Jews that had already travelled to or through British and other western port cities.

The barely established Jews faced a threat to those freedoms and rights which port Jews had previously gained because of the fear of disease carried by those newly arriving from the Baltic – and the port of Libau in particular.

Though Riga retained a larger Jewish community than Libau, and although it could be said that it had a greater influence upon Jewish enlightenment than the latter port, the Jews of Libau undoubtedly held a unique position in commercial affairs within and without absolutist Russia during the end of the nineteenth and beginning of the twentieth centuries.

The Poor Jews' Temporary Shelter
If there was a waiting period between their arrival at a British port and their departure elsewhere, immigrants were forced to stay in temporary lodging houses. After 1885, poor Jewish migrants arriving in London increasingly stayed in the Poor Jews' Temporary Shelter in Aldgate. Most of the surviving registers of the shelter have been computerised and can be searched at
<http://chrysalis.its.uct.ac.za/shelter/shelter.htm>
Other migrants may have stayed at other forms of charitable or commercial shelters as described by Nicholas J Evans: *A roof over their heads* in *Shemot* (the journal of the JGSGB), March 2001.

Passenger Lists
The **Hamburg Passenger Lists** on-line cover the period 1850-1905 and copies can be ordered via the Mormon Family History Libraries. Lists for the years 1850 to 1934 have been almost completely preserved in the Hamburg State Archives. The lists were created in Hamburg (the port of embarkation) when the passengers left from there. Currently only those records for the period 1890-1905 are on-line, but further records are being added continually. The ultimate aim is to have all the lists available on-line. The lists contain details of direct services to the US and Canada, as well as lists of passengers travelling indirectly via Britain. Both lists are indexed.

<http://linktoyourroots.hamburg.de/>

There are no records for passengers arriving in the UK, except for those arriving before 1869 (HO3) or who appear as leaving Hamburg on an indirect steamship service via Britain. Passenger lists have survived for those emigrants leaving Britain 1878-1888 and 1890-1960. These are held at the **National Archives** Kew in London. They are listed by the British port of departure and found within the records of the Board of Trade (BT27). The lists have not been indexed and can only be searched at the National Archives. If you have the date of departure and name of the vessel on which your ancestor left Britain, then the task of searching for a particular vessel is not too difficult.

Records for the steamship and railway operators who ran such services have not survived. On-line guides to the passenger records of the PRO can be found at
<http://www.nationalarchives.gov.uk/default.htm>

American Passenger Lists are available from the National Archives in the USA. Indexes to them are available for certain ports and time periods, and the passenger manifests are also available on microfilm. Both the microfilmed indexes and the manifests may be consulted at the National Archives in Washington, DC, and in several regional branches throughout the US. The LDS Family History Library has microfilm copies of all indexes and manifests held by the National Archives, which are available on loan at local Family History Centres.

Information on holdings in the US National Archives and Records Administration (NARA) of interest to genealogists may be found at
<http://www.archives.gov/>
NARA also has booklets on the subject of genealogy. Another reference is: Coletta, John Philip, *They Came in Ships* (Salt Lake City, Ancestry, 2nd ed, 1993).
Ellis Island   <http://www.ellisisland.org/default.asp>
Steve Morse   <http://www.stevemorse.org/>

Information on holdings in the US National Archives and Records Administration (NARA) of interest to genealogists may be found at
<http://www.archives.gov/ >

Other Sources of Information
YIVO Institute for Jewish Research
Archives and Library
Centre for Jewish History
15 West 16th Street, New York, NY 10011
Tel: +1 212 246 6080 - Fax: +1 212 292 1892
E-mail: vivo1@metgate.metro.org

Web site: <http://www.yivoinstitute.org/>

YIVO's holdings are unique, and staff assistance is usually required. Call or e-mail in advance for an appointment to do research. There are some holdings about Latvian Jews. There is also a booklet called A *Guide to YIVO's Landmanschaften Archive* by Rosaline Schwartz. See also: Mohrer, Fruma and Web, Marek, *A Guide to the YIVO Archives*, M. E. Sharpe, N.Y., 1998.

Groups of people from the same town organised themselves into mutual aid groups called **Landsmanschaften**. An example of this was the Kurlander Young Men's Mutual Aid Society (KYMMAS). A list of its members may be found on the Latvia SIG website. There are a number of books published on Landsmanschaften for particular cities (e.g. New York and Chicago), and information may be found about organisations of members from Latvian areas.

Other repositories that may be of help in New York include:
American Jewish Historical Society, American Jewish Joint Distribution Committee Archives, American Sephardi Federation, Brooklyn Public Library - Brooklyn Collection, Center for Jewish History Genealogy Institute, Hebrew Immigrant Aid Society, Jewish Theological Seminary of America Library, Leo Baeck Institute, Municipal Archives, National Archives, New York City Board of Elections - Manhattan, New York County Clerk - Division of Old Records, New York Public Library Map Division, Queens Library - Long Island Division, Tamiment Library and Robert F. Wagner Labor Archives, Yeshiva University Museum.

THE HOLOCAUST IN LATVIA

Riga was occupied on 1 July 1941, and its ghetto was established on 25 October. Bloody events began on 28 November.

The 1935 census recorded 94,000 Jews in Latvia. Of these, 4,000 left the country before the Soviet occupation of July 1940, when 5,000 were promptly deported to Siberia. A further 15,000 fled to the Soviet interior ahead of the Germans, leaving a Jewish population of 70,000 in 1941. Only 3,000 survived. The Jews died in three stages: between July and October 1941, 34,000 from the provinces and Riga were murdered; at Rumbula, 27,000 were killed in the first week of December 1941; between January and July 1942, 14,000 more died. In addition to those in Kaiserwald, Rumbula and Salaspils, there are reputed to be 60 mass grave sites.

The **Extraordinary Commission Records for Latvian Towns**[12] was established by the Soviet Union after World War II to investigate German-Fascist crimes committed on Soviet Territory. Vadim Altskan of the United States Holocaust Memorial Museum has helped Latvia SIG with details of the records, which are arranged by locality.

TOWN	VICTIMS	LOCALITY	TOWN	VICTIMS	LOCALITY
Abrena	120		Neritas	41	Jekabpils
Aizpute	187		Pampal	7	Kuldiga
Atashinski	16	Rēzekne	Panemune		Bausk
Dagda	320	Wollust	Plavinas	38	
Dagda	585		Preli	165	
Eglan	80	Daugavpils	Pridruysk	446	Daugavpils
Gostinii	80		Ramkas	10	
Griva	60		Rēzekne	45	
Ilvi	68		Rēzekne	23	
Indra	88		Riebenishki	234	
Indra	137		Riga	450	Proletarian
Ishawa	24		Riga	2500	
Izwalte	50	Daugavpils	Rupsk	15	Jelgava
Jekabpils	330		Silani	17	
Jelgava	51		Skruntzen	12	
Kaplava	25		Valgamas	130	Liepāja

TOWN	VICTIMS	LOCALITY	TOWN	VICTIMS	LOCALITY
Kavnatski	30		Valmi	54	Limbazi
Krāslava	120		Varklani	160	
Kuldiga	72		Viesitska	220	Jekabpils
Limbazi	114		Vikenovski	20	
Livani	450		Vilani	368	
Ludzia	195		Vishki	500	Daugavpils
Medeny	30	Jekabpils	Zaiyin	32	Jekabpils

Yizkor books (memorial books) were written by survivors of a given town. They tell about the town's history and usually give lists of Holocaust victims. Many have been translated. See <http://www.Jewishgen.org/databases/yizkor> and *Jewish Memorial (Yizkor) Books in the United Kingdom – Destroyed Jewish Communities* by Dr. Cyril Fox and Dr. Saul Issroff. ISBN: 0 9537669 5 0. Published in 2006 by the JGSGB.

Information received from US Holocaust Memorial Museum Washington[13] is contained in the following filmed reels of Stutthof concentration camp (RG 04.058M). The lists are generally in alphabetical order and include both Jews and non-Jews.

Reel 287 (end of reel) Almaleh. Moise - Bellet, Jean
Reel 288 Atlas, Lewa - Kirsch, Salman
Reel 289 Kirschbaum, Hanna - Günters, Peter
Reel 290 Gureckis, Ausis - Millers, Alfred
Reel 291 Mincenko, Valerians - Schittler, Alfons
Reel 292 Schewiskows, Wladislaus - Vitols, Emdja
Reel 293 Wainstock, Abram -Zweinicks, Walis

There are names of other Latvian Jews and Latvians scattered throughout this collection of 305 reels of film but they are difficult to locate.

Prof. Edward Anders born in Liepāja has made major contributions to Latvian research relating especially to Jews from Liepāja formerly Libau.

<http://muse.jhu.edu/demo/holocaust_and_genocide_studies/v017/17.1anders.html>

Lists other than those of the Extraordinary Commission which may be of interest are:

Leonid, Koval, *Book of salvation*, 2 vols.
(Koval is President of the Society of the Genocide Studies and History of the Ghetto.)
Volume 2: *Jurmala, Latvia* includes a list of Jews from various Ukrainian communities who died in the Holocaust. Some entries include birth dates. Pp.174-183 includes a list of physicians who died in the Riga ghetto; entries include date of birth, university attended and death date. Pp. 183-192 includes list of medical students who died in the Riga Ghetto.

List of Jews transported from the camp Ereda, Estonia to Riga, Latvia (26 March 1944), compiled 7 August 1945. Entries include occupation, last residence. (USHMM Archives - 1997 A. 0235, reel 2, file 50/12)

Alphabetical list of Jewish survivors in Dvinsk, Latvia. 60 names. Entries include year of birth. (USHMM Archives - 1997 A. 0235. Reel 6, file D56/19).

Alphabetical list of Jews in Riga, Latvia of 15 May 1945 200 names. Entries include father's name, present address. (USHMM Archives – 1997 A. 0235, Reel 6, file D56/22)

Alphabetical list of Jews in Riga, Latvia 2 June 1945. 150 names (USHMM Archives - 1997. A. 0235, Reel 6, file D56/22)

Concentration camps[14] were located in the Riga area and elsewhere. Larger camps included those at Salaspils and Kaiserwald (Meza Parks). The Salaspils camp, set up at the end of 1941, contained thousands of people, including many Latvian and foreign Jews, especially from Lithuania. Conditions in this camp, one of the worst in Latvia, led to heavy loss of life among the inmates.

The Kaiserwald concentration camp, established in the summer of 1943, contained the Jewish survivors from the ghettos of Riga, Daugavpils, Liepāja and other places, as well as non-Jews.

At the end of September 1943, Jews from the liquidated Vilna ghetto were also taken to Kaiserwald. When the Soviet victories in the summer of 1944 forced a German retreat from the Baltic States, the surviving inmates of the Kaiserwald camp were deported by the Germans to Stutthof concentration camp near Danzig, and from there were sent to various other camps, mostly to Dachau.

After the German defeat, 13,000 Latvian Jews returned, mainly to Riga. Over 20,000 others from the Soviet Union joined them. By 1970, almost 37,000 Jews were living in Latvia. Some returned to be reunited as families. Latvia, even under Soviet rule, was better than in Russia. Riga had a Jewish population of 30,000, the balance settling in Daugavpils, Liepāja and smaller towns. Riga in particular became a centre of revived national awareness and agitation. It was there that the movement of Jewish identity affiliated to Israel began. This initiative inspired a spirit of affirmation that stirred Jewish communities throughout Eastern Europe and the western world.

Some Gentiles assisted in saving Jews. Jan Lipke helped to save several dozen Jews of the Riga ghetto by providing them with hideouts. 1,000 Latvian Jews survived their internment in concentration camps; most of them refused repatriation and remained in the displaced persons camps in Austria, Germany and Italy. Along with the rest of the survivors they eventually settled in new homes, mostly in Israel. In Latvia itself, several hundred Jews had somehow managed to survive. A public demonstration was held in Riga a few days after its liberation, in which 60 or 70 of the surviving Jews participated.

Useful address:
Jewish Survivors of Latvia, Inc.
74 Short Way
Roslyn Heights, NY 11577, U.S.A.
Tel: + 516 625 0210

CEMETERIES

Jewishgen has a large World Cemetery Database online. See <http://www.Jewishgen.org/databases/cemetery>. In 2006 photos will be included in the present listings for Jekabpils cemetery.

The International Association of Jewish Genealogical Societies sells a Cemetery CD-ROM, which contains details of cemeteries throughout the world, including Latvia. Avotaynu sells cemetery data on microfilm. The cemetery data listed here is a compilation from various sources such as Aleksandrys Feigmanis (historian and genealogist), Rita Bogdanova (Latvian State Historical Archives), Latvia SIG newsletters and personal visits to cemeteries.

Cemeteries with Jewish tombstones are:

AIZPUTE (Hasenpoth): The cemetery was almost completely destroyed but about 100 tombstones remain. Many date from the early 1800s.

BAUSKA (Bauske): The Jewish cemetery was destroyed in the 1960s.

DAGDA: Fewer than 100 tombstones remain.

DAUGAVPILS (Dvinsk): The oldest cemetery was destroyed and no longer exists. The next oldest was totally destroyed by the Soviets in the 1970s. There are only a few old tombstones, including those of some famous rabbis that were transferred into the Daugavpils Jewish cemetery. The new cemetery has a few hundred stones, and some Jews are buried in a special part of the Christian cemetery. There may be 70 years of cemetery records in existence.

GOSTINI (Dankere/Glazmanka): The cemetery is located in a forest and there are fewer than 200 tombstones remaining.

JAUNJELGAVA (Friedrichstadt): A very large and old cemetery still exists. There are many nice tombstones with artistic engravings of lions, birds, etc.

JEKABPILS (Jacobstadt): The cemetery is still used a little by the present small Jewish population. It is not maintained, but is not completely overgrown. All the remaining tombstones have been photographed by Aleksandrys Feigmanis who was requisitioned to do this by Arlene Beare on behalf of Latvia SIG. The tombstone photos have been scanned by Arlene Beare. The database and photos have been donated to The Jewishgen Online Burial Registry-JOWBR and can be accessed at
<http://www.Jewishgen.org/cemetery>

JELGAVA (Mitau): The cemetery was founded in the 16th century and almost totally destroyed in Nazi and Soviet times. There are about 30 tombs but these have no tombstones. Only four legible tombstones remain.

KRĀSLAVA: The cemetery dates from the 1600s and is in good condition. In the post-war section there are three markers with 52 names of the Jewish soldiers from Krāslava who died while serving in the Red Army.

KRUSTPILS The old cemetery was destroyed in abt. 1970, but all old stones were moved to the new site. About 300 stones still remain.

KULDĪGA (Goldingen): The old cemetery has sections belonging to different faiths. The grounds are well maintained as a park, but relatively few marked graves remain. The Jewish section has about 40 tombstones, some with engravings dating back to the 1820s.

LIEPĀJA (Libau): The cemetery is in relatively good condition and was not destroyed in the War. It is combined with a Christian cemetery and about 500 tombstones remain. Between 25 and 36 books contain records of all burials since 1909. Jewish burials end in 1941.

PILTENE (Pilten): One of the oldest and most picturesque cemeteries of Latvia, it has tombstones starting in the 17th or 18th century.

PREILI (Preil): The cemetery is well maintained.

RĒZEKNE (Rēzhitze): The cemetery is in the suburbs of the city and is in good condition. The oldest tombstones date from the middle of the 19th century. About 300 stones remain.

RIGA: The old Jewish Cemetery, which is totally destroyed, was at 2/4 Liksne Street and is now a park, with a memorial stone to show that it was once a Jewish cemetery. The new cemetery, founded in 1920, has thousands of tombstones. The guardian of Riga cemeteries has the list of all funerals since 1951.

SALDUS (Freuenburg): The cemetery is in very bad condition.

SHMERLI: Many Jews who returned and whose relatives were buried in Russia and other places have relocated their graves to this large Jewish cemetery.

SKAISTKALNE (Schonberg): The cemetery is quite large and there are about 40 very nice tombstones.

SUBATE: The cemetery is about 200 years old. It is neglected and the local (non-Jewish) community have at times shown an interest in maintaining it.

TALSI (Talsen): The cemetery is located opposite the Christian cemetery. It is overgrown but some tombstones remain. Some of the graves have been vandalised.

TUKUMS (Tukkum): This cemetery is in good condition but only half the original 400 tombstones remain. The cemetery is due to be replaced with a paved road.

VALDEMARPILS (Sassmacken): The Jewish cemetery is east of the town centre on a wooded hillside overlooking Lake Sasmaka. Little remains of it: there are two small gravestones and one tomb.

VARAKLANI: The cemetery is in good condition with more than 250 monuments remaining. The oldest tombstone dates from the 1820s.

VENTSPILS (Windau): About 40 interesting tombstones still exist.

VILJANI (Marienburg): A small cemetery still exists.

Jekabpils Jewish cemetery © Arlene Beare

MUSEUMS AND LIBRARIES

Museum in Bauska:

The Local Lore and Arts Museum of Bauska
(Bauskas novadpeetnieciibas un maakslas muzejs)
6 Kalnu Str., Bauska, LV-229300 Latvia
Aigars Urtans, Mag. Hist.,
Tel: +371 3922651

Museums in Riga:

Jewish Museum (Museum and Documentation Centre-Jews in Latvia)
Skolas Street 6, LV-1322, Riga, Latvia

The Jewish Community Centre is in the same building. Here one finds the Jewish community, as in any country in the world, making parcels of clothes or food for those in need as well as holding social functions.

Museum of History of Riga and Navigation

4, Palasta Str., Riga, LV-1050, Latvia
Tel: +371 7211358

There are a few small Jewish items.

Museum of Photography

Marstalu iela 8, Riga, LV-1050, Latvia,
Tel: +371 7222713 and +371 7227231
E-mail: Lvfoto@lanet.lv

Latvian National Library

Scientific department of rare books and manuscripts
6/8 Jekaba Street, Riga
Tel: +371 7223881

Jewish books and periodicals and other sources (some in Yiddish) can be found here.

Latvian Academic Library

10 Rupnieciibas Str., Riga
Tel: +371 7106206

Some Jewish periodicals and other materials.

Latvian Occupation Museum (1940-1991)

Strelnieku laukums 1
Riga LV-1050
Tel: +371 721-2715   Fax: +371 722-9255
Email: omf@latnet.lv

LATVIA AND THE INTERNET

The Jewishgen Latvia Database
The search for roots on the Internet should start at the Jewishgen page <http://www.Jewishgen.org>

You will need to register with Jewishgen in order to search any of the Databases or to join a Discussion Group.

To register yourself with Jewishgen, go to the **Jewishgen New User Registration** form at-

<http://www.Jewishgen.org/cure/jgidadd.asp>

Complete the form fully and accurately, and then press the "Register as a New Jewishgen User" button at the bottom of that page.You will then be sent an **acknowledgement email message**.

From the Jewishgen main page click on the link to the JGFF "Jewishgen family finder", which is under the heading "Research". If you wish to search the JGFF then click on "Search" and enter your family name. You will see a drop-down menu: choose "Sounds like" (Daitch Mokotoff Soundex) rather than "Exact Spelling" search. You will be prompted to enter your Email address and password.

You have to be registered with Jewishgen to do a search of any Database. The Soundex will bring up all the variations of spelling. There are three boxes: "name", "shtetl", "country". The modern spelling of the shtetl is the only one that will be recognised. If you are unsure of the modern name then either check in the book *Where Once We Walked* by Gary Mokotoff and Sallyann Amdur Sack or from the main page under "Research", go to the Jewishgen Shtetl Seeker.

The Jewishgen Latvia Database is a great source of information for Latvian researchers.
<http://www.Jewishgen.org/databases/latvia>

Useful starting points for research relating to Latvia:
Latvia SIG page
<http:www/Jewishgen.org/Latvia>
Courland page
 <http://www.Jewishgen.org/courland>
Riga page
<http://www.Jewishgen.org/riga/rigapage.htm>
Jekabpils page
<http://www.Jewishgen.org/jekabpils/jekabpils.htm>

The Jewishgen Latvia Database (formerly the All Latvia Database) is a combined effort of the Latvia SIG and the Courland Area Research Group. The excellent introductions to the databases on the web were written by Constance Whippman. Databases are added at regular intervals.

The Component Databases can be found at-
<http://www.Jewishgen.org/databases/latvia>

Clicking on the title of each database gives details of how the database was compiled. If you wish to do a search then there is a search box at the top of the page above these names and you can enter the surname or the name of a town. The exact spelling may be entered or you may enter "sounds like" which will bring up permutations of spelling and sound. (Daitch-Mokotoff Soundex Search)The next page will show how many hits there are in each database and you can then check all the hits to see if any of the results relate to your ancestors. It is important to check all the hits in the different databases because as I have said previously our ancestors moved around a lot.

Component Databases on the Web as at the end of 2005

Latvia:

Jewishgen Family finder
There are over 7,000 entries by Jewish genealogists researching families in Latvia.

Jewishgen Online Worldwide Burial Registry
This database contains over 1,000 burial records for Latvia and Latvian Landsmanschaft cemeteries worldwide.

The All Russia 1897 Census-Latvia
The database has detailed family data for over 7,000 individuals living in Riga; Rēzekne and Krustpils (Vitebsk gubernia); and five towns in Courland, as recorded in the "All Russia Census" of 1897. There is an ongoing project to extract all surviving material from this important source.

The 1897 All Russia Census is one of the most important sources for research throughout the Russian Empire. This census has 16 headings including place of origin which is of the greatest importance in your research. This database is particularly valuable because it takes a great deal of time for the Archivists to find a family as the lists are not in alphabetic order but are listed by address. Latvia SIG has an ongoing project to add to this database and at present the list contains data from Riga, Rēzekne, Krustpils, Talsi, (formerly Talsen), Jaunjelgava, (formerly Friedrichstadt), Jekabpils, (formerly Jakobstadt), Valdemarpils, (formerly Sassmacken) and Tukums.

Jewish Religious Personnel in the Russian Empire
Listed are 420 Jewish religious personnel from Kurland, Livland and Vitebsk gubernias.

Livland Gubernia:

Jewish inhabitants of Riga 1885.1886

A database of 2650 entries, both male and female, listed as lawfully residing in Riga in or about 1885. Reference is made to over 4000 individuals.

The Police compiled lists of 2646 Jews registered as living in Riga in 1885/1886. The original list, organised by suburb and district of residence, was a comprehensive inventory of Jewish families. The Jews were considered a separate Hebrew nationality ("Ebraier") and like other foreign nationals were registered with the police authorities. Unfortunately the lists only survive in part, so that there would have been substantially more adult Jews living and working in Riga than appear here. The surviving sections of the list now form part of the holdings of the Latvian State Historical Archives in Riga. They are hand-written in Cyrillic, with some German annotation. Taking into account the fact that the list includes reference to the father's name as well as the person registered, there are over 4,000 named individuals referred to and in many cases two generations.

Riga Tax Administration List

A database of 12,000 entries, male and female, taken from the Riga Tax Administration records compiled and amended during the years 1858-1917. There are references to over 23,000 individuals living and working in Riga.

This database of some 12,859 tax administration records for 1858-1917 was created as an alphabetical register in Riga in 1904 to assist in the collection and administration of taxes. It is a composite list, in that it incorporates information from previous tax lists, in particular those of 1858-1887. Following the creation of the 1904 list, the archivists continued to add new information as late as 1917. The list includes fathers' names in 10,826 cases, so that there is genealogical information about not less than 23,685 individuals and information concerning two generations of the same family in over 20,000 cases. Some 2,100 maiden names are listed, providing important information about maternal lines.

The Extraordinary Commission Lists:Riga

There are over 2,000 individuals who were residents of Riga and are recorded as having perished at the hands of the German forces, most during 1941.

The Extraordinary State Commission was formed to investigate and Establish War Crimes of the German-Fascist Invaders and record the fate of Nazi victims. Over 2000 names of Riga victims have been extracted from the records and donated to Latvia SIG by Vadim Altskan of the USHMM. A project is planned to compile a large list of Latvian Jewry known to have perished between 1941 and 1944.

Riga Passport and Travel Documents Registration List 1900.

This list has Information on over 12,500 individuals from throughout the Russian Empire, who resided temporarily in Riga in 1900 and registered their presence and travel documents with the police. (details page 30)

Jewish marriages in Riga, 1854-1921

This is an index from a register of 9,241 marriages dating from 1854-1921. There are nearly 20,000 given names and surnames listing the names of both the bride and groom. The database comes from an alphabetical register of 9,241 marriages in the Latvian State Historical Archives in Riga. The list was compiled in Russian, probably at the beginning of the 20th century. The marriages date from 1854-1921.The database contains only the names of the bride and groom (surname and given name) and the year of marriage. All further information must be obtained from the Archives in Latvia. Note that some names of bride and groom are missing, because the name does not appear in the original records.

How do you obtain these Jewish Marriage Records?
The records up to 1905 are held by the Latvian State Historical Archives.

You must write to: Ms. Irina Veinberga, Head of Department
Latvian State Historical Archives
Slokas iela 16
Riga LV-1048
LATVIA
E-mail: irinwein@latnet.lv.

The records from 1906-1921 are held at:
The Archives of the Registry Department
Kalku Street 24
Riga LV-1050
LATVIA

The Latvian State Historical Archives will provide copies of documents with translations into English or German, whereas the Archives of the Registry Office do not provide copies, but just give the detailed report in Latvian. The usual cost of a record from the Latvian State Historical Archives is about 10 dollars, but they will let you know how much to send. The Archives of the Registry have to bill through the Consular Department of the Ministry for Foreign Affairs. After you contact them with a request for a document they will let you know how much it will cost and where you have to make payment. The Latvian Embassy in your country will notify you that the documents have arrived and you can send them the money.

Courland Gubernia:

The Courland 1907 Duma voters list
There are names of 3,300 males eligible to vote in the 1907 Russian Duma elections in twenty of the major towns and villages of Courland gubernia, including entries for the 1905 list of Jewish voters of Windau. References are made to nearly 5.900 individuals.

Recruits Enlistment Registers and Family Lists
Included are names of adult family members extracted from official Jewish military recruits enlistment registers from ten major cities of

Courland, together with an 1874 family census list from Bauska. The list contains some 8.000 entries and over 11,000 named individuals.

Passlossen-Jews without Lawful permit
A list of 990 Jews without a lawful permit (Passlossen) published in the official Government gazette, the *Vedomosti*, in the Summer of 1855.

Jews in Hasenpoth(Aizpute) 1834
A database of over 1,000 male Jews lawfully entitled to reside in Hasenpoth taken from material microfilmed in the Riga Archives in 1941.

The Courland Vedomosti Database
There are over 2,000 entries giving details of news reports and listings from the official Russian News Gazette from Kurland between the years 1853-1860.

Vitebsk Gubernia

The Dvinsk (Daugavpils) Family Lists
This is a very large database of over 8,200 entries providing some 14,000 names of members of the Jewish community of Dvinsk, Vitebsk gubernia. The list includes excerpts from merchant's lists, lists of petit bourgeois, tax and military recruit's lists.

This is a large Dvinsk database of over 8,000 names of inhabitants of Daugavpils (Dvinsk) 1878-1915, and is made up of lists of petty bourgeois families. It was created in 1881, 1882, 1884 and 1885 by the petty bourgeois head of Dvinsk, its police officer and tax clerk. The lists were set up on orders of the Dvinsk City Council for tax and military service purposes. Family lists were first created in 1876 and supplemented up to 1917. They contain extensive information about families and include details of relationships over a few generations that may be unlisted. The Merchants' List was set up in 1876. All of the original records were in Russian.

Jewish Families of Rēzekne
A database of 6,600 entries of members of the Jewish community of Rēzekne (Rezhitse, Rositten). Detailed information is provided on each family from 1898.

1911 Vsia Rossiia business directory-Vitebsk
Data for 3,611 businesses in Vitebsk gubernia from the 1911 "All Russia" business directory.

Latvia SIG also has the following acquisitions-

Riga voter's lists 1877, 1882, 1886, 1901, 1905, and 1913.
Riga business advertisements 1910/11
Riga Telephone directories 1923/24 and 1934/35
Courland Business Directory 1892/93
First Livland doctors 1905
Latgale doctors and lawyers 1910/11
Latgale address book for homes and businesses 1920
Latgale Trade and Industry Directory 1926
Rēzekne Business Directory 1923/24
Riga Polytechnic students/ Tartu University Graduates 1889-1918.
Tallinn Business Directory 192

Acquisitions and contributions of the Courland Research Group
3

This is an active and enthusiastic group with a special research interest in Courland. Their primary purpose is to promote the study of the history of the Jewish communities of Courland and Latvia generally and to work with other professionals in the fields of Jewish studies and history with the shared aim of understanding the intellectual and social history of the Jews of Courland.

The Herder Film Project
Unfortunately, unlike Lithuania, Estonia and Poland, it has not been the policy of the State Historical Archives in Riga to permit archive documents or lists to be copied by the Church of Jesus Christ of Latter Day Saints (Mormons) for preservation. At present there is no indication that this policy is likely to change. However, some material is available on microfilm through the Mormon Family History Centres, which was acquired indirectly.

In 1940/41 the Baltic Germans microfilmed archival material in the Historical Archives at Riga prior to their retreat from Latvia in 1941. The microfilm was taken back to Germany where it was eventually lodged at the Herder Institute, Marburg, Germany. The Institute permitted the Mormons access to this film in the 1980s when copies were made and lodged as part of their collection. This is potentially a valuable source of material for Jewish families of Courland from 1795 to 1834.

After extensive negotiations the Herder Institute agreed to sell a set of these films to the Courland Research Group and they are now working actively with both the Herder and the LDS to create an index to all Jewish entries. The list of the Jews of Hasenpoth (Aizpute) is already available and can be searched on-line through the Jewishgen Latvia Database.

Jewish Military Recruits enlistment registers and family lists
Extracted from official Jewish Military Recruits Registers and family lists from the major cities and towns of Courland including Friedrickstadt (Jaunjelgava), Libau (Liepāja), Goldingen (Kuldiga), Grobin (Grobina), Tuckum (Tukums), Pilten (Ventspils), Jakobstadt (Jekapils) and Bausk (Bauska). The database contains 12,500 named entries.

Gubernski vedomosti
Courland, in common with most other provinces of the Russian Empire, published its own government-based official gazette with public announcements, reports of legal cases, commercial activity, lists of those with tax arrears or escaping from the draft, news of special Jewish interest such as the appointment of synagogue officials, and property sales. All entries of Jewish interest have been indexed between the years 1853-1860. This database includes approximately 2,500 entries. It is hoped that this can be extended to the vedomosti published for Livland province, which included Riga, and that eventually the database will act as an index to Jewish material up to 1900.

Schools and education database

The Courland Research Group is particularly interested in the history of education in Courland and other areas of Latvia. To date they have collected and put into databases lists of donors to the Herder Schools in Riga, 1914, with names and addresses of donors and an education charities list from 1925 (over 2,000 entries).

Old directories are providing the names of teachers in the Jewish schools and headmasters from the major towns. A Higher Education and University database is nearly complete and will hopefully be fully searchable on-line by the time this booklet is printed.

Courland Jews had access to university level education without quota at the Riga Polytechnical Institute, which attracted Jews from throughout the Russian Empire as well as from Courland. Lists survive from the Latvian University Jewish Associations including some photographs and career details. There are lists now available from Tartu University, which will be included.

Voter Lists

Databases have been completed of all persons eligible to vote in the 21 towns and cities of Courland from the 1907 Duma elections. Although the percentage varied from town to town, it was fairly typical that over 30% of voters were of Jewish origins. Many families had emigrated by 1905, but details of those remaining provide important information about towns of origin and other social detail.

Business directories and telephone books

Business directories were published for Courland and, after independence, for Latvia as a whole. Although relatively few homes had telephones, especially in rural areas, telephone directories are a valuable resource for those families and businesses that are included because they also provide address information. Here are Latvian telephone directories for 1928 and 1940 and numerous private directories listing householders and business owners from 1882, 1912 and other years. The first stage of the project is under way to catalogue the existing Vsia Rossia directories from the late 19th century for the major towns in Courland.

Passlosen 1854-1858
Jews without lawful permits, published in the summer of 1855.

The doctors of Courland 1825-1900, by Issidorus Brennsohn
This book, published in Mitau in 1904, provides biographies of about 125 doctors with Jewish connections.

Jewish Religious Personnel in Russia, 1853-54
This database is a searchable list of over 4,000 synagogue employees from 900 towns in the Pale of Settlement.

Tukums community pre-1941
Martha Lev-Zion translated this memoir by an unknown author. It describes the structure, activities and participants in the Jewish community of Tukums in the early 20th century, and serves as a yizkor book for this community.

Shtetlinks
You may find helpful information if your shtetl has a shtetlink page. These may be accessed from the main page by going to "Shtetlinks", which you will find under "Projects and Activities"; click on Latvia.
You may also access the site direct by going to
<http://www.shtetlinks.Jewishgen.org/Latvia.html>

Shtetlinks currently listed on the shtetlinks page:

Dagda, Jekabpils, Kuldiga (Goldingen), Liepāja, Ludza, Riga, Subate and Varaklani.

Off site resources:
Daugavpils and Riebini

URLs that may be useful

All Lithuanian Database	<http://www.Jewishgen.org/litvak/all.htm>
Belarus SIG	<http://www.Jewishgen.org/belarus/>
Courland Area Research Group	<http://www.Jewishgen.org/courland>
Cyndi's List	<http://www.cyndislist.com/>
Jewishgen	<http://www.Jewishgen.org/>
Jewish Genealogical Society of Great Britain	http://www.jgsgb.org.uk>
Latvia SIG	<http://www.Jewishgen.org/latvia>
Poland Homepage	<http://www.Jewishgen.org/jri-pl/>
Poor Jews Temporary Shelter	<http://chrysalis.its.uct.ac.za/shelter/shelter.htm>
Riga	<http://www.Jewishgen.org/shtetlinks/riga/rigapage.htm.>
Riga in your Pocket	<http://www.inyourpocket.com/Latvia/index.shtml>
USA Holocaust Museum	<http://www.ushmm.org/>
LDS Mormons	<http://www.familysearch.org>
Maps	<http://www.feefhs.org/maps/indexmap.html>
Search engine	<http://www.google.com>
Avotaynu	<http://www.avotaynu.com>
Rootsweb	<http://www.rootsweb.com>
Ancestry com	<http://www.ancestry.com>
Yad Vashem	<http://www.yad-vashem.org.il/>
Cemetery Database	<http://www.Jewishgen.org/Cemetery>
Latvian Genealogy	<http://www.roots-saknes.lv/mainroots.htm>
Latvian Gen Jews	<http://www.roots-saknes.lv/Ethnicities/Jews.htm>

SPECIAL INTEREST GROUPS

Latvian SIG UK (hosted by JGSGB)

Members of The Jewish Genealogical Society of Great Britain are welcome to be members of the Latvian SIG UK (Special Interest Group). This UK Special Interest Group must be differentiated from the Latvia SIG hosted by Jewishgen.

Latvia SIG (hosted by Jewishgen)

The Latvia SIG is a Special Interest Group hosted by Jewishgen with a membership fee of US$20 for US residents and US$30 for overseas. Details can be found on the Latvia SIG Web page, <http://www/jewishgen.org/latvia>. All Jewishgen services such as newsgroups and access to Jewishgen Web sites are free. The subscription is for the quarterly hardcopy newsletter and also to assist in the acquisition of data for the All Latvia Database and for other SIG projects. The newsletter contains interesting articles that are very helpful as an aid to your search. You may also wish to contribute an article.

Discussion group (newsgroup)

Latvia SIG and Courland Area Research Group each have a discussion group, as do all SIGs.

Many members are unclear as to how to subscribe to the group and post messages. Discussion groups provide a helpful forum for exchange of ideas and information. There are often so many messages on Jewishgen that it is easy to miss messages with a specific Latvian interest.

How to Subscribe

From the Jewishgen home page click on Discussion Groups. You will be taken to a page-
<http://www.Jewishgen.org/Jewishgen/DiscussionGroup.htm>
Under contents on the right you click on subscribe. You will be required to enter your Email address and Password to subscribe to a Discussion Group. If you have not yet registered click on "I am a new user and want to register." Once registered, fill out the form.

Select the SIG to which you want to subscribe and click on "submit the form" which is an automated process. If you do anything incorrectly the program notifies you instantly. You will receive an e-mailed request to confirm your subscription and all you need do is click on the reply button and it will be sent back to the proper address. You will get a welcome document from the SIG and it will give you the address to which you send all messages.
<http://lyris.Jewishgen.org/ListManager/>

There are **Jewishgen discussion group message archives**, which you may find particularly useful as you can search all the messages that have ever been posted on the Discussion Group. From the Jewishgen homepage click on Discussion Group Archives

From the **Riga homepage** you may link to information on:
Jewishgen Latvia Database (formerly All Latvia Database)
The Jewish Museum of Riga
Centre for Judaic Studies at the University of Latvia
The Holdings of the Latvian State Historical Archives (Inventory only)
Kibbutz Shefayim inventory
Ancestors' photos
Photos of Riga

The **Courland Research Group homepage** links to information on:

Jewish Religious Personnel in Russia, 1853-54
> This is a searchable list of over 4,000 synagogue employees from 900 towns throughout the Pale of Settlement.

HaMelitz **Lithuanian and Latvian Donors, 1893-1903**
> A searchable list of almost 20,000 Lithuanian and Latvian charity donors, listed in this Hebrew periodical.

ShtetLinks

Jewishgen's compendium of links to web pages devoted to particular towns or communities. Pages of interest include ones for Dvinsk, Goldingen, Jakobstadt, Libau, Sassmacken, Subbat, Talsen and Tukums.

Yizkor Books

Jewishgen's collection of Yizkor books devoted to particular towns or communities contains very little on Courland, exceptions being the books for Libau and for the Poperwahlen concentration camp. In addition, a translation is available of the entry for Libau from the Pinkas HaKehilot, the encyclopedia of Jewish communities.

Latvian Subscription List Database

A browsable list assembled by Harold Rhode for Latvia SIG from several sources: subscription lists appearing in books published during the 19th and early 20th centuries denoting sponsorship of the authors; names from the index of the book *Di geshikhte fun di Idn in Letland fun yor 1561-1923 [History of the Jews in Latvia]*, published in 1928 in Riga; contributors to agricultural communities in present-day Israel and Syria.

State Department Riga Consulate Records, 1924

A browsable list assembled by Mike Getz for Latvia SIG, from records of Diplomatic and Consular offices of the U.S. Department of State, presently located in the National Archives II facility in College Park, MD.

Kurlander Young Men's Mutual Aid Society

A browsable list assembled by Naomi Freistadt for Latvia SIG, recording the names, dates of birth, towns of origin and names of spouses, where available, of members born in Latvia. The period covered stretches from the 1870s to the 1920s and later.

Poor Jews' Temporary Shelter Database, 1895-1914

The Poor Jews' Temporary Shelter in London was the temporary home of many east European Jews on their way to their new homes abroad. Jews from Latvia and Lithuania en route to the US and South Africa are disproportionately well represented.

A database has been constructed at the University of Leicester under the leadership of Professor Aubrey Newman and Dr. John Graham Smith, based on the Shelter registers between 1895 and 1914. The development of the database, and analysis of the records, is described in a paper. The database can be searched on the web site of the Kaplan Centre for Jewish Studies and Research at the University of Cape Town.

1941-1945 Libau Victims and Survivors

Edward Anders and colleagues have assembled a remarkably complete listing covering almost all the 7,100 Jews who lived in Libau in June 1941. This searchable database includes family relationships, addresses, dates of birth and death, and numerous other sources of genealogical data in the tragic story that it tells. Dr. Anders has made available to the Courland Research Group the complete list of surnames represented in his database, as well as a separate list sorted alphabetically by maiden names.

1930s Libau Business and Property Owners

This is a list of Paul Berkay's 1938 Libau property owners' list and 1930 Libau business owners' list, along with other links to Libau information.

Latvian Jews Executed during the Stalin Era

A Russian-language on-line database lists more than 2000 Jews who lived in Moscow and were executed during the Stalin era. A list of about 100 of these having Latvian roots is provided here; it was extracted and translated by Stanislav Gorbulev.

Travel in Latvia

If you are making your first visit to Latvia, the following information may be of help to you in finding your way around:

Major airlines fly to Riga and you are recommended to check with your travel agent as times and dates of departure may vary. Flights leave from Heathrow and Gatwick. There is a one- or two-hour time difference from the UK depending on the time of year.

Latvia Guides and Researchers

Jewishgen has a policy of not recommending guides or researchers. However should you require a guide on your trip to Latvia you will need someone totally familiar with the various shtetlach and their Jewish past as well as the cemeteries.

Aleksandrys Feigmanis is a guide, cemetery researcher and genealogist for Latvia, Lithuania and Belarus. He may be contacted by e-mail: aleksgen@mailcity.com or through his web-site: <www.balticgen.com>. He also speaks English, Latvian and Russian as well some French.

It is important to discuss the cost of his services before engaging him either to take you around or to do Research. I cannot be held responsible for any inaccuracies in the research done on your behalf. Should you have any queries about the research you will need to verify the results with the Latvian State Historical Archives.

Guide books in English
Baltic States by Lonely Planet ISBN 981-258-157-X
Guide to Latvia, Bradt Publications, UK (Globe Pequot Press Inc, USA)
Latvia a Guide Book by Ouse Plus Ltd can be purchased in Riga at a bookstore.
Riga in your Pocket is an inexpensive booklet that has helpful information and is usually for sale in your hotel.
Riga and its Beaches, Farrol Kahn Landmark Publishing Ltd

Currency/banks
Currency can be purchased at the airport on arrival. The currency is now in Euros as Latvia is part of the European Union. Lats will no longer be legal tender after 2008. The exchange is open until late at night and can be visited on arrival before you go through passport control. Banks are plentiful in Riga and there are cash points for obtaining money with a credit card.

At the time of writing there are about 9,000 Jews in Latvia, nearly all in Riga. They are not all original inhabitants as many came from Russia and elsewhere after the War. Inter marriage was common. A head of community presides over a committee. The community centre is at 6 Skolas Street. Services are held in the Synagogue at Peitavas Street on Shabbat and High Holy Days.

Reproduced with permission from the Lonely Planet website
www.lonelyplanet.com © 2005 Lonely Planet Publications

Transport/touring

Buses are easy to use. The taxis are not always of a very high
standard, but in general they are fine. The main roads are in a
reasonably good condition.

When touring outside Riga it is a good idea to take drinking water and
some food, as there are very few places to obtain refreshments.

It is a preferable to have someone with you who can speak Latvian or
Russian as very little English is spoken outside Riga.

Riga Sightseeing with a Jewish Interest

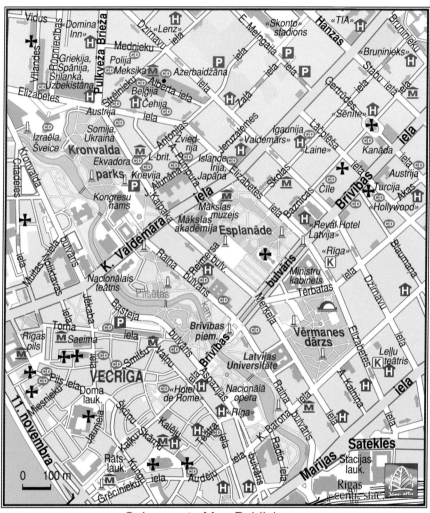

© Jana seta Map Publishers.

Start your tour in **Alberta iela** (iela is a street) near top of map and slightly off centre to the left.

Alberta Street where **Isaiah Berlin** lived has some beautiful Eisenstein facades. Mikhail Eisenstein (1867-1920) was the father of the famous film director Sergei Eisenstein. Although his origins were German-Jewish he was a member of the Orthodox Church in Riga. He designed 19 buildings in Riga.

Plaque on house in Alberta Street where I. Berlin was born.
© Arlene Beare

Sir Isaiah Berlin was born in Riga in 1909 and died in the United Kingdom in 1997. In 1915 the family moved to Petrograd and from Petrograd to England in 1921. Sir Isaiah Berlin was a pupil of St Paul's school and then studied at Corpus Christi College, Oxford. He was a world renowned Philosopher, was awarded many prizes, and was preoccupied with free will and determinism.

Eisenstein Façade Alberta iela 2a © Arlene Beare

91

After leaving Alberta iela walk down Antonias iela to Elizabetes iela. Turn left along Elizabetes iela and after crossing Vademara turn left into Skolas iela where the Jewish Community Centre housing the Jewish museum is situated at number 6 Skolas iela. A moving video presentation of the Holocaust in Riga can be seen there. The exhibits display life in Riga as it used to be.

You can walk to the **Old City (Vecriga)** from Skolas iela. In the Old City there are interesting old buildings but not really much of Jewish interest. However one cannot visit Riga and not visit the Old City with its cobble stones and early architecture.

Walk along Elizabetes Street and turn right down Brivibas Street.

Art Deco Building © Arlene Beare

The French Embassy © Arlene Beare

This beautiful Art Deco building is located at Raina Blvd 9. Walking down Brivibas you cross Raina Blvd and if you turn left you will find the **University of Latvia** located on the left side. The **Centre for Jewish Studies** is in the University building and Prof Ruvin Ferber would be happy for you to visit the Centre. There is not much for you to see as there is only a small Library and an Office. The books are in Latvian, Russian or German with few exceptions.

I have created a page for the Centre and attached it to my Riga page. You can access the page and read about the Centre for Judaic Studies.
<http://www.shtetlinks.Jewishgen.org/riga/LV_univ.htm>

The Centre hosts a Conference "Jews in a Changing World". The last Conference was a few years ago and the next one, the sixth, will be
September 11-14, 2006
University of Latvia Main Building, center for Judaic Studies,
Riga, LV-1586, Latvia Email: jsc@latnet.lv

The Freedom Memorial is in the Park as you walk down Brivibas from Raina Blvd towards the Old Town.

Freedom Monument on way to Old Town © Arlene Beare

Opera House in the Park © Arlene Beare

The Opera House is well worth a visit if you love opera or ballet. Book your seats ahead of your visit at the Latvia National Opera webpage: <http://www.lmuza.lv/opera/default.asp>

Riga Old Town © Arlene Beare

Riga Old Town © Arlene Beare

The Peitavas Street Synagogue is in the Old City of Riga.
The Synagogue at Peitavas 6/8 has a number of members, although few come regularly. More come for the High Holy Days. One can visit the Synagogue at any time.

Interior of Synagogue at Peitavas Street (1997) © Arlene Beare

After leaving the Old City take a taxi to the **Jewish Memorial Stone in the Park** near the Moscow Road and continue down the Moscow Road on foot.

Old Jewish cemetery now a Park © Arlene Beare

The **Old Jewish Cemetery** at 2/4 Liksnas Street is now a park. All that remains is a memorial stone with an inscription. The old cemetery was the first piece of land that the Jews acquired in Riga. Prior to the 18th century they had to take their dead to Poland and later to a Jewish cemetery near Mitau (now Jelgava) in Courland.

The **New Jewish Cemetery** at 4 Lizuma Street, Shmerli is another taxi ride. This cemetery dates from the 1920s.

From the memorial in the park walk down the **Moscow Road** where one can still see old houses that may have been the homes of Jews.

Moscow Road © Arlene Beare

Old Jewish Houses in Moscow Road. © Arlene Beare

Bikur Cholim Hospital, Moscow Road © Arlene Beare

The Hospital is in need of funds but still manages to perform a great service to the community. Moscow Road and the surrounding streets mark the old Moscow suburb that became the **Riga Ghetto.**

A **Chabad Jewish School** is at 141 Lacplesas Street. It is worth going in to see what a wonderful education the children are receiving. Rabbi Mordechai Glazman is the Headmaster.

There is an enormous **Central Market** with five old hangars filled to capacity with meat, fish, bread and many other items. This is definitely worth a visit and is not far from Moscow Road.

Central Market © Arlene Beare

There are the remains of the **Big Choral Synagogue** at 25 Gogola Street that was burnt down with Jews inside on July 4, 1941. This was the largest and most beautiful of the Riga synagogues. The synagogue was famous for its singers, both cantors and choir. Non Jews also came to the synagogue on Jewish holidays to listen to the outstanding cantors. About 300 Jewish refugees from Lithuania had taken shelter in the synagogue and together with Jewish families from the neighbourhood and passers-by were burnt to death. A memorial stone was inaugurated here on July 4, 1988.

Ruins of Old Synagogue at Gogol Street © Arlene Beare

Memorial Stone to the Jews murdered in the Synagogue
© Arlene Beare

Outside Riga
If you are planning a visit outside Riga then it is well worthwhile finding out if there is a Jewish community. There is not much left to see of the Jewish past other than the occasional old building. Check the cemetery lists to see if there is a cemetery in the shtetl you would like to visit. There is usually a street that may be identified as having had Jewish inhabitants and possibly old Jewish houses. It is recommended that you take someone who speaks Russian or Latvian when touring outside Riga.

Depending on your special interest there are other places to visit such as Liepāja, Rumbula, Jurmala, Tukums, Jelgava, Jekabpils, Daugavpils, Bauske and Rēzekne. Jurmala and Tukums are well worth a visit. Jurmala is an attractive seaside resort where the Russians had beautiful dachas. Tukums is an old shtetl of Courland.

Skede Memorial Liepāja © Rita Bogdanova

Street in Tukums with old Jewish Houses © Arlene Beare

Street in Jekabpils where Jews lived © Arlene Beare

Grave stones in Tukums old Jewish cemetery © Arlene Beare

Liepāja (Libau) on the west coast is the important port from which our ancestors left Latvia. Ventspils and Piltene are also in the west, and Piltene has a large picturesque cemetery with old gravestones.
Sigulda, NE of Riga, is in the Gauja National Park, as are Valmiera and Cesis. One may see the old castle at Sigulda as well as the Turaida Museum. The historical name of Latvia, Livonia, is derived from the Livs who inhabited a large part of Vidzeme and Kurzeme. The museum has exhibits depicting the history and craftsmanship of the Livs.

Part of Skede memorial Liepāja © Rita Bogdanova

Rumbula

© Rita Bogdanova

Rumbula memorial

Rumbula Forest, near Riga, Latvia, became the mass murder site and grave of approximately 25,000 Jews from the Riga Ghetto on November 30 and December 8, 1941 (10th and 18th of Kislev on the Jewish calendar). The dedication of the Rumbula memorial took place on November 29, 2002 where there was a moving ceremony of remembrance. A very beautiful website dedicated to Rumbula with photos of Latvia can be found at <http://www.rumbula.org>

Bikernieki Forest

Approximately 40,000 Jews from throughout Europe were murdered at Bikernieki Forest and are buried there. In 2001, a fitting memorial was dedicated at this site on the outskirts of Riga, Latvia.

© Rita Bogdanova

Bikernieki Memorial Stone

© Rita Bogdanova

The Inscription on the Memorial Plaque reads:

HERE, IN THE FOREST OF RUMBULA ON NOVEMBER 30 AND DECEMBER 8 OF 1941 THE NAZIS AND THEIR LOCAL COLLABORATORS SHOT DEAD MORE THAN 25,000 JEWS PRISONERS OF THE RIGA GHETTO – CHILDREN, WOMEN, OLD PEOPLE, AS WELL AS AROUND 1,000 JEWS DEPORTED FROM GERMANY. IN THE SUMMER OF 1944 HUNDREDS OF JEWISH MEN FROM THE CONCENTRATION CAMP "RIGA--KAISERWALD" CAMP WERE KILLED HERE.

SHETLACH MODERN LATVIAN AND OLD GERMAN/RUSSIAN NAMES

The modern Latvian name of the shtetl is important, as it is the name that appears on the maps. When doing a Jewishgen search on the Internet it is important to enter the modern spelling.

LATVIAN (now)	OLD NAME	LATVIAN (now)	OLD NAME
Aizpute	Hasenpoth	Piltene	Pilten
Alūksne	Marienburg	Plavinas	Stockmannshof
Ape	Oppekaln	Preili	Preil
Bauska	Bauske	Rēzekne	Rositten/Rēzhitze
Cēsis	Wenden	Sabile	Zabeln
Daugava	Dvina	Saldus	Frauenburg
Daugavpils	Dvinsk	Siguidas	Segewold
Dobele	Doblen	Skaistkalne	Schonberg
Gostini	Dankere *(Glazmanka)	Slokas	Schlock
Grobiņa	Grobin	Smiltenes	Smilten
Gulbene	Schwanenburg	Talsi	Talsen
Jaunjelgava	Friederichstadt	Tukums	Tukkum/Tuckum
Jekabpils	Jakobstadt	Valdemarpils	Sassmacken
Jelgava	Mitau	Valmiera	Volmar
Kandava	Kandau	Ventspils	Windau
Krustspils	Kreutzburg	Viesite	Eckengraf
Kuldīga	Goldingen	Vilaka	Marienhausen
Liepāja	Libau	Vilāni	Wilon/Welonen
Ludza	Lutsin		

Griva was a separate shtetl not far from Daugavpils.
It is now a suburb of Daugavpils so you will not find it on a map.

Gostini was also known as Ventelburg in German.
*Please note that Glazmanka was the Russian name.

LATVIAN LANGUAGE

According to the Latvian and Lithuanian Language Guide, (Lonely Planet - Baltic States Phrase Book) they are the only two surviving languages of the Baltic branch of the Indo-European family. Because many of its forms have remained unchanged longer than those of other Indo-European languages, Lithuanian is very important to linguistic scholars. Latvian and Lithuanian share quite a lot of words, but are not quite close enough to each other to be mutually intelligible. They separated from each other around the 7th century AD.

Latvian Language:
The letters in the Latvian alphabet are usually pronounced as in English, except for the following:

c	is pronounced **ts**	č	is pronounced **ch**
ġ	like the **j** in **jet**	j	like the **y** in **yes**
ķ	like **tu** in **tune**	l	like the **lli** in **billiards**
o	like the **a** in **water**	š	as **sh**
ž	like the **s** in **pleasure**	a i	like the **i** in **line**
e i	like the **ai** in **main**	i e	like the **ea** in **rear**
ā	is pronounced like the **a** in **barn**	ē	is pronounced like the **a** in **care**
ī	is pronounced like the **e** in **she**	ū	is pronounced like the **oo** in **hoot**

In Latvian and Lithuanian the days of the week are often abbreviated to their first one or two letters in timetables etc. It is important to recognise the difference between PR (Monday) and P (Friday) in Latvian and Lithuanian. Saturday and Sunday in Latvian would be SV (Sunday) and S (Saturday) and in Lithuanian S (Sunday) and Š (Saturday).

ENGLISH	LATVIAN	ENGLISH	LATVIAN
Monday	Pirmdiena	Address	Adrese
Tuesday	Otrdiena	Age	Vecums
Wednesday	Trešdiena	Date of Birth	Dzimšanas datums
Thursday	Ceturtdiena	Name	Vārds
Friday	Piektdiena	Place of Birth	Dzimšanas vieta
Saturday	Sestdiena	Sex	Dzimums
Sunday	Svētdiena	Surname	Uzvārds

ENGLISH	LATVIAN	ENGLISH	LATVIAN
January	Janvāris	Marriage	Laulïbas, Precïbas
February	Februāris	Divorce	Laulïbas, Škiršana
March	Marts	Cemetery	Kapsēta
April	Aprīlis	Property	Manta, Ïpašums
May	Maijs	Inheritance	Mantojums, Iedzimtïba
June	Jūnijs	Town	Pilsēta
July	Jūlijs	Townhall	Rātsnams
August	Augusts	Library	Bibliotēka
September	Septembris	Jewish	Ebrejiete (f)/Ebrejs (m)
October	Oktobris	Family	Gimene
November	Novembris	Do you	Via jūs runāj at
December	Decembris	speak	Angliski?
		English?	

ENGLISH	LATVIAN	ENGLISH	LATVIAN
One	Viens	Nine	Deviņi
Two	Divi	Ten	Desmit
Three	Trīs	Twenty	Divdesmit
Four	Četri	Thirty	Trīsdesmit
Five	Pieci	Forty	Četrdesmit
Six	Seši	Fifty	Piecdesmit
Seven	Septiņi	Hundred	Simts
Eight	Astoņi	Thousand	Tūkstotis

ENGLISH	LATVIAN	ENGLISH	LATVIAN
Grandchild	Mazbērns	Brother-in-law	Svainis
Granddaughter	Mazmeita	Sister	Māsa
Grandson	Mazdēls	Sister-in-law	Svaine
Grandfather	Vectēvs	Mother	Māte
Grandmother	Vecāmāte	Mother-in-law	Vīramāte
Son	Dēls	Father	Tēvs
Son-in-law	Znots	Father-in-law	Vīratēvs
Daughter	Meita	Niece	Brāļameita Māsasmeita
Daughter-in-law	Vedekla	Nephew	Brāladēls Māsasdēls
Brother	Brālis	Cousin	Brālēns

FAMOUS JEWISH LATVIANS

The spiritual and religious life of Israel was influenced by a number of Latvian rabbis (Abraham Isaac Kook, Mordechair Nurok, Joseph Rosen and Meier Simcha). This is not a comprehensive list and merely records a few famous Latvians.

Avigur, Shaul b. 1899 Daugavpils (Dvinsk), d. 1978 Israel. One of the organisers and first leaders of Hagana. Director of Mossad le'Aliya Bet 1944-1948. From 1953 leader of the movement for the repatriation of Soviet Jews to Israel.

Berlin, Isaiah (Sir) Author and philosopher, came from Riga.

Berlin, Mendel Father of Isaiah.

Don-Yahia, Yehuda Leib 1869-1941. Rabbi from Latgale. Went to Israel in 1936. One of four rabbis who formed the Mizrachi movement.

Dubin, Mordechai   Leader of Latvian Jewry in 20th century Latvian Parliament, 1920-1934. Arrested in 1941 and deported to Russia. d. 1956.

Dubnow, Simon   Famous historian, murdered by the Nazis at Rumbuli.

Gulak, Asher (Prof)   b. 1881 Dakira, near Riga, d. 1940 Jerusalem. Lived near Riga, went to Israel in 1925. In 1936 became a professor at the Hebrew University in Jerusalem. A historian of Talmud law.

Kook, Abraham Isaac ha Cohen   b.1865,   Griva,   d.1935, Jerusalem

Outstanding rabbinical authority, studied at Volozhin Yeshiva 1884-1886. Rabbi in Zheimeli, Lithuania 1886. Rabbi in Bauska, Latvia 1895. Moved to Palestine in 1904, Rabbi of Yaffo. Went to Europe 1914, first Switzerland, then London in 1916. Back to Palestine 1919, first Ashkenazi Chief Rabbi for Palestine 1921.

Mikhoels, Solomon   b. Dvinsk. Studied law in St Petersburg. After further study became an eminent actor in the Soviet Union, achieving great fame as King Lear. Brutally killed in Minsk 1948. This was the first step in the liquidation of all Jewish culture in Soviet Russia.

Nurok, Mordechai   b. 1879 Tukums, d. 1962 Tel Aviv. Rabbi in Jelgava (Mitau). One of the founders of World Jewish Congress, active leader of Mizrahi movement. Member of Saeima (Latvian parliament) in inter-war Latvia. Went to Israel in 1947.

Rosen, Joseph   The Rogachover, b. 1858 Rogachev, Byelorussia, d. 1936 Vienna, buried in Daugavpils. Famous Hasidic authority, leader of Hasidic community in Daugavpils.

Rosowsky, Boruch Leib   1841-1919. Riga's famous cantor, pupil of the even greater Sulzer, took synagogue music forward to great heights within its traditional framework.

Rosowsky, Solomon b.1878 Riga, d.1962 New York. Son of Boruch Leib, Jewish composer. Eminent musicologist and music teacher in Israel where he began his life's work, *The Cantillation of the Bible.*

Simcha, Meier haCohen   1843-1926, famous talmudic authority in Daugavpils (representing mitnagdim), active supporter of the Zoinist idea.

Old Synagogues

In Sabile, Tukums and Kuldiga - there are no Jews and synagogues are used for other purposes, mostly cultural. The Kadish synagogue in Daugavpils was recently reopened after reconstruction. In Rezekne there is the Green Synagogue.

Frequently asked Questions (FAQs)

- Can you put me in touch with a researcher in Latvia?
Page 86

- How do I access data in the Jewishgen databases?
Page 70

- How do I obtain a Jewish marriage record?
Page 75

- How do I obtain records for birth, marriage or death after 1905? Page 75

- What is the address of the Latvia State Historical Archives?
Page 23

- Can I write to the Archives in English? Yes. Page 23

- When do I contact a Local Registry Office in Latvia?
Page 43

- Do I need the exact town where my ancestor came from?
Page 16

- How do I place a message about my family on the Internet?
Page 82

- Where was the Vitebsk Gubernia? Page 44

- Is it appropriate to offer the ladies at the Archives (or anyone else I email with genealogy questions) some remuneration for their searches? You just need to pay the requested fee for the Archives. A thank you is all that is necessary if you ask a question and receive an answer.

- Who were the Petty Bourgeois? Petty Bourgeoisie is a lower middle class, special category of the city inhabitants.

Petty bourgeois paid taxes and were taken as recruits (merchants were not recruited).
The archivists do not know why they were known as "petty" but of course in English it means trivial or inferior. According to the Oxford English Dictionary- A Bourgeois was originally a French citizen or freeman of a burgh as distinguished from a peasant and a gentleman. Now it means a member of the mercantile or shopkeeping middle class of any country.

- I understand there is a seminar for the Jews of Riga?
  "Jews in a Changing World" Conference
  Center for Judaic Studies
  University of Latvia
  19 Rainis Blvd
  Riga, LV-1586, Latvia
  E-mail: < jsc@latnet.lv>
  The next one will be September 11th -14th 2006

- How do I become a member of the Latvia SIG? Page 82

- Do I have to pay to be a member of a Discussion Group? No

- How do I obtain back issues of the newsletter? Write to the Treasurer Mike Getz mikegetz005@comcast.net

- Do I need to send a fee when I request research from the Archives? Page 23

- Nurmusen pag., Talsen d. what is "pag."? Pag means pagasts - volost - small rural district

- When did the Jews of Latvia take surnames? Page 17

- Where do I find the modern name of the Shtetl? Page 16

- Where did our Ancestors from Latvia go when they left Latvia? Page 54

BIBLIOGRAPHY FOR LATVIA AND COURLAND

NB: Where known, the whereabouts of a book has been indicated by a symbol for the library concerned thus:

BL   British Library
JC   Jews' College Library (London School of Jewish Studies)
JGSGB   The Jewish Genealogical Society of Great Britain's Library at 33 Seymour Place, London, W1H 5AU
SSEES   School of Slavonic & East European Studies, University of London
STN   Southampton University – Parkes Library
UCL   University College London Jewish Studies Library
WL   Wiener Library, London

Avtsinsky, Levi
Toldot yeshivot ha-Yehudim be-Kurland mi-shenat 321(1561) and 668 (1908). Vilna: (s.n.), 672, 1912
(Series: Hebrew books from the Harvard College Library; HI 0041-0042)
Berman, Shevach
Lo halakh ba-telem. Tel-Aviv: Y. Golan, 1995. Survivor's story of a Riga Jew
Beider, Alexander
A Dictionary of Jewish Surnames from the Russian Empire. **JGSGB**
Bobe, Mendel
Perakim be-toldot Yahadut Latviyah 1651-1918, 'arikhah, Y. Har-Even. Tel Aviv: Reshafim, c.1965.
Bobe, Mendel
The Jews in Latvia. 1971. **JC**

Buchholtz, Anton
Geschichte der Juden in Riga bis zur begrundung der rigischen Hebraergemeinde im j. 1842. Riga: N. Kymmel, 1899. **SSEES**

Cohen, Chester
Shtetl Finder, Gazetteer. Names and location of Shtetls in the Pale of Settlement. Includes Latvia. **JGSGB**

Debrer, Maria
Riga - a Guide. **JGSGB**

Dribins, Leo
Ebreji Latvija. Riga: 1996, **BL**

Dvinsk (Daugavpils)
Le-zekher kehilat Dvinsk (hukhanah 'a. y. kitot 8/1-8/2 be-hadrakhat ha-morah Tamar Amarant). Hefah: Hativat Benayim 'Kiah', (1974). A short (63 page) yizkor book for Dvinsk (Daugavpils).

Dvinsker bundisher brentsh 75, Arbeter Ring: 35-yoriker yubiley zshurnal: 1904-1939. New York: Arbeter Ring, 1939?
(Subject: Workmen's Circle Dvinsker brentsh 75-Anniversaries, etc.)

Eliyav, B
Latvia: Yahadut Latvia. Sefer Zikaron. 1953

Ezergailis, Andrew
The Holocaust in Latvia, 1941-1944

Feldmann, Hans
Verzeichnis lettlandischer Ortsnamen 1963
A dictionary of Latvian place names and their German equivalent. It has both German-Latvian and Latvian-German.
This is also available from the FHC - film number 0496720 (item 5)

Flior, Yudel
Dvinsk; the rise and decline of a town. Translated from the Yiddish by Bernard Sachs. Johannesburg: Dial Press 1965. **UCL**

Foner, Sarah Feige (Meinkin)
Mi-zikhronot yeme yalduti 1903.
The author's recollections of Dvinsk (Daugavpils) between 1862 and 1871, written in very old-fashioned Hebrew, mentions prominent families in Dvinsk.

Huttenbach, Henry
Introduction and guide to the Riga Ghetto

Iwens, Sidney
How dark the heavens: 1400 days in the grip of Nazi terror. New York: Shengold Publishers, c.1990

Jussmann, Max
Les bottes du Tzar, Paris: Editions municipales, 1993. A genealogy of the Jussmann family of Riga

Kacel, Boris
From Hell to Redemption. Boulder: University Press of Colorado, 1998

Katz, Josef
One who came back: the diary of a Jewish survivor, translated from the German by Hilda Reach. New York: Herzl Press; Bergen-Belsen Memorial Press, c.1973

Kaufmann, Max
Die Vernichtung der Juden Lettlands: Churbn Lettland. Muenchen: The Author, 1947. **JC UCL**

Latvia Synagogues and Rabbis
1918-1940 **JGSGB**

Levin, Dov
Pinkas ha-kehilot. Latviyah ve-Estonyah: entsiklopedyah shel ha-yishuvim ha-Yehudiyim le-min hivasdam ve-'ad le-ahar Sho'at Milhemet ha-'olam ha-sheniyah, 'orekh, Dov Levin, be-hishtatfut Mordekhai Naishtat. Yerushalayim: Yad va-shem, rashut ha-zikaron la-Sho'ah vela-gevurah, 1988
Register of the Communities. Latvia and Estonia, edited by Dov Levin.
Le-zekher kehilat Dvinsk, (hukhanah 'a. y. kitot 8/1-8/2 be-hadrakhat ha-morah Tamar Amarant). Hefah: Hativat

Levinstein, Meir
'Al kav ha-kets. (Tel Aviv): Moreshet Bet 'edut 'al shem Mordekhai Anilevits': Sifriyat po'alim, 735, 1975

Libau (Liepāja)
A Town Named Libau. Israel: 1985?
(no publisher name, total of 36 pages, 25 in English, 2 in German, 9 in Hebrew, with a name index)
A yizkor book for Libau (Liepāja), a copy of which is available in the library of the JGS of Greater Washington, located in Rockville, MD. An on-line translation is available (Jewishgen Translations)

Mark, Mendel
Di Yidish-veltlekhe shul in Letland. NYU-York : Tsiko, 1973

Mikhelson, Frida
I survived Rumbuli, translated from the Russian and edited by Wolf Goodman, 1979. **JC**
Ovcinskis, L
(Toldot ha-Yehudim be-Kurland. Yiddish.)
Di geshikhte fun di Idn in Letland. 1928
Press, Bernhard
Judenmord in Riga. 1941-1945. Berlin: B. Press, 1988
Punga , Astrida & Hough, William
Guide to Latvia, Old Saybrook, 1995
Schneider, Gertrude
Journey into terror: story of the Riga Ghetto. New York: Ark House, c.1979
Schneider, Gertrude
The Riga ghetto, 1941-1943. New York: 1973
Schneider, Gertrude
The Unfinished Road: Jewish survivors of Latvia look back. New York: Praeger, 1991. The final volume of Gertrude Schneider's trilogy. Survivors' stories of Latvian Jews (mostly from Riga) and Jews from other parts of Europe who spent time in Latvian ghettos and labour camps, including Kaiserwald, Dundaga and Salaspils. Includes photos and an index of names.
Sherman-Zander, Hilde
Zwischen Tag und Dunkel: Madchenjahre im Ghetto. Frankfurt am Main: Ullstein, 1984. Series: Ullstein Buch; Nr. 20386.
Tseitlin, Shmuel
Dokumental'naia istoriia evreev Rigi. Izrail': (s.n.), 1989
(Translation: Documentary History of Riga Jews)
Tsilevich, L et al
Evrei v Daugavpilse: istoricheskie ocherki, Daugavpils: Daugavpilsskaia evreiskaia obshchina, 1993. (Translation: Jews in Daugavpils: Historical Essays.)
The best book about Jews in Daugavpils (Dunaburg/Dvinsk). **BL**
Vesterman, Marger
The Jews in Riga: Fragments of the Jewish history of Riga. **JGSGB**
Volkovich, B
Ravviny v Daugavpilse (1920-1940). Daugavpils: 1996

Zil'berman, David
I ty eto videl. New York: Slovo-Word, 1989 (Translation: And you saw it)
Zvonov, M.
'Po evreiam - ogon'!' (Riga: s.n.) 1993
(Translation: 'To the Jews - Aim - Shoot!')

Microfilms

Regesten und Urkunden zur Geschichte der Juden in Riga und Kurland (microform), herausgegeben von der Rigaer Abteilung des Vereins zur Verbreitung von Bildung unter den Juden in Russland ...fg. 1-3. Riga: Die Abteilung, 1911-1912.

Rigasches Adressbuch. Salt Lake City: Gefilmt durch The Genealogical Society of Utah, 1963. This is a microfilm of the 1914 city directory for Riga. Written in German Fraktur script, it is divided both by street name, and by surname. (LDS Microfilm 0477271)

Journal & maps in JGSGB Library

Journal - Latvia SIG. A Journal of Jewish Genealogy in Latvia, Jan. 1996 to date

Map - Estonia, Latvia, Lithuania - Contemporary road atlas – indexed, 1:300,000 1994/5

In Russian and Latin type. City street plans of: Kaliningrad, Riga, Tallinn and Vilnius, Estonia, Lithuania and Latvia. Town plans of Riga, Tallinn and Vilnius.

Wiener Library – extra list of Holocaust books

List of Jews residing in Riga
Kovno - The burning ghetto (yiddish), Shmuel Galbort
Partisans of the Kovno ghetto. Dmitri Galpernius. Vilnius 1969

The Doctors of Courland 1825-1900, by Issidorus Brennsohn

This book, published in Mitau in 1904, provides biographies of about 125 doctors with Jewish connections.

Jewish religious personnel in Russia, 1853-54

A searchable list of over 4,000 synagogue employees from 900 towns throughout the Pale of Settlement.

A Selection of Latvian Books listed as being held in Yad Vashem Archive Library, Jerusalem, Israel

Akzin, Benjamin
Choices before the Baltic States. New York: Council on Foreign Relations, 1937

Apse, Jan
The Baltic States. London: Pallas, 1940
Latvia in 1939-1942: background, Bolshevik and Nazi occupation, hopes for future. Washington, DC: Press Bureau of the Latvian Legation, 1942
Latvia under German occupation in 1943. Washington: Latvian Legation, 1944

Avotins, E
Daugavas Vanagi: Who are they? Riga: Latvian State Publishing House, 1963

Berzins, Alfred
The unpunished crime. New York: R. Speller, c.l963

Crowe, David M
The Baltic States and the Great Powers: Foreign relations, 1938-1940. Boulder: Westview Press, c.l993

Daugavas Vanagi
Who are they? Riga: Latvian State Publishing House, 1963

Duhanovs, Maksims
1939: Latvia and the year of fateful decisions. Riga: University of Latvia, c.1994

Eksteins, Modris
Walking since daybreak. A story of Eastern Europe, World War II, and the heart of our century. Boston, MA: Houghton Mifflin, 1999

Ezergailis, Andrew
The Holocaust in Latvia 1941-1944: The missing center.
Riga: The Historical Institute of Latvia.

Gordon, Frank
Latvians and Jews between Germany and Russia. Stockholm: Memento, c1990

Hesse, Ingeborg
Sascha: A story of love and survival. Sydney: Bantam Books, c.1991

Hiden, John ed.
The Baltic and the outbreak of the Second World War.
Cambridge University Press, c. l992

Jundzis, Talavs ed.
The Baltic States at historical crossroads: Political, economic, and legal problems in the context of international cooperation on the doorstep of the 21st century. Riga: Academy of Sciences of Latvia, 1998
Kacel, Boris
From hell to redemption: A memoir of the Holocaust. Niwo. University Press of Colorado, c.1998
Kalme, Albert
Total terror: An expose of genocide in the Baltics. New York: Appleton-Century-Crofts, c.1951
Latvia Legation U S A
Latvia under German occupation 1941-1943. Washington, DC: Latvian Legation. Press Bureau, 1943
Levin, Dov
Arrests and deportations of Latvian Jews by the USSR during the Second World War. Charleston, 11. The Association for the Study of the Nationalities USSR and Eastern Europe, 1988
Levin, Dov
Baltic Jews under the Soviets, 1940-1946. Jerusalem: Centre for Research and Documentation of East European Jewry, Avraham Harman Institute of Contemporary Jewry, Hebrew University of Jerusalem, 1994. JC
Levenstein, Meir
On the brink of nowhere. Albany, New York
Levinson, Isaac
The untold story. Johannesburg: Kayor Publ. House, 1958 JC
Meiksins, Gregory
The Baltic riddle: Finland, Estonia, Latvia, Lithuania key-points of European peace. New York: L. B. Fischer, c.1943
Plakans, Andrejs
Historical dictionary of Latvia. Lanham, MD: Scarecrow Press, 1997
Press, Bernhard
The murder of Jews in Latvia, 1941-1945. Evanston, 11: Northwestern University Press, 2000
Ratz, Jack
Endless miracles. New York: Shengold, 1998

Silabriedis, J
"Political refugees" unmasked! Riga: Latvian State Publishing House, 1965

Vestermanis, Margers
Fragments of the Jewish history of Riga: A brief guide-book with a map for a walking tour. Riga: Museum and Documentation Centre of the Latvian Society of Jewish Culture, 1991

Winter, Alfred
The Ghetto of Riga and continuance. Monroe, CT: 1998

PART II
ESTONIA

History

The Estonians have closer linguistic links with Finland than the Latvians but both countries have had foreign rulers from the 13th to the 20th century. The name derives from Aestii, used by the Romans in 100 BC, describing tribes east of Germany. The second language is Russian and English is increasingly spoken.

There is evidence of a Jew called Johannes Jode living in Tallinn in 1333. In the 16th century Jews were not allowed to live in Estonia and Livonia. The Cantonists founded the Estonian Jewish community and according to verbal tradition their first illegal community. A prayer house already existed in Tallinn in 1830. Young Jewish boys aged 8-11 were raised in the Russian Orthodox faith in military units. During the Crimean War the Nicolai Soldiers with their families were settled in Estonia; these were Jewish soldiers who had been drafted into the Russian army for 25 years. There were 60-80 families in Tallinn in 1856 and approximately ten families each in Tartu and Parnu (Pärnu) in 1859. Regular Jewish communities were created later; in 1884 they were expelled from the regions not belonging to the Jewish Settlement Area but were permitted to remain if they had arrived prior to 1879.[15]

The first documents in the archives mentioning Jews date from 1786, in connection with an agreement to permit a small number to settle in Tallinn. By 1820 the number had increased to 36. As a community, Jews did not live in Tartu until 1866 when 50 Jewish families arrived and established a prayer house. (Tartu is now in south Estonia but up to 1917 was in Livland.) A little later, Jewish prayer houses also opened in other south Estonian cities: in 1882 in Pernov (now Pärnu) and Arensburg (now Kuressaare), and in 1891 in Valk (now Valga).

The 1846 census states that 5,265 Jews were living in the province of Curonia (Courland) and 524 in Livonia. Official Russian documents of the 19th century state that persons confessing to be Jewish were forbidden to settle, form communities or open synagogues in Estland up to 1856. Nevertheless some Jews lived in Estland before that time; these were foreign and baptised Jews, illegal traders from Poland and Lithuania and vagrant Jews. [16]

The province of Estonia was throughout the Swedish and early Russian occupation, a summer resort for the nobilities of those countries and was completely closed to Jews. Nicholas I and his government devised the cruel and demonic plan to cause the Jews to assimilate in the early 19th century. By the time of WW2 the community had peaked to about 4,500 souls spread out through Tallin, Tartu, Valga, Parnu, Narva, Rakvere, Viljandi and Voru as well as small family groups in a further 8 townlets. During the first Soviet occupation a considerable number of the well to do Jewish "enemies of the State" were deported to Siberia, thereby having their lives saved from the Germans. With the German invasion many more Jews fled into Russia, those that remained behind were slaughtered to the last man or were deported to the camps. The numbers varied between 1,100 and 1400 and the German commander in Estonia was able to report that Estonia was "Judenrein" clear of Jews. Thus about 60% were in fact saved by the Soviets.

Those that had been deported, mostly to Siberia, were forced to sign an agreement to remain there for a long period to help in the Russian effort to populate Siberia. When the war was over many of the Jews gravitated back to Estonia, some legally others not. Some of the latter were hounded and either forced to flee or were arrested and deported back to whence they had come. As the Russian administration eased up after Stalin many Jews from other areas were encouraged to settle in Estonia in a Soviet effort to *Russify* the province. By the time of "Perestroika" there were 5,000 Jews in the country, the only country in the Eastern block that had a Jewish population greater than its pre-war one. With the opening of the gates to Jewish emigration, large numbers left for the west or for Israel. In fact most of the Estonian part of the community moved to Israel leaving behind altogether a population of around 1500. [15]

PROVINCES OF ESTONIA	JEWISH INHABITANTS	
	1897	1934/ 1935
Tallinn (North-Estonia -Russian province Estland 1710-1918)	1191	2203
Rakvere	89	100
Haapsalu	18	5
Paide	4	18
Narva - in 1897 member of province of Peterburg	474 Pervaja vseobschaja perepis' naselenija. T. XXXVII. S.-Peterburgskaja gub. P. 262-263. Community since 1877, EHA documents from 1898	188
Tartu (South-Estonia - Estonian Livland, Russian province Livland 1710-1918	1760 Do, T.XXI Lifljandskaja gub. P.76-77	920
Valga	380	262
Võru	258	96
Viljandi	166	121
Pärnu	396	248
Kuressaare	30	22
Nõmme (Estland - North -Estonia)	-	75
Paldiski	1	1
Türi	-	2
Põltsamaa	-	2
Tapa	-	9
Tõrva	-	1
Petseri (1918-1940 Estonia)	-	4
	Total in town 4763	Total in town 4277

ESTONIA

Estonian Towns

NEW	OLD	NEW	OLD
Abja-Paluoja	Abia (Vietingsgut)	Paide	Weissenstein
Antsla	Anzen	Paldiski	Rogerwiek Baltischport Port Baltiysky
Elva	Elva	Põltsamaa	Oberpahlen
Haapsalu	Hapsal	Põlva	Põlve -Pölve
Jõgeva	Laisholm	Pärnu	Pernau
Jõhvi	Jewe	Püssi	Püssz Neu-Isenhof Uue-Purtse
Kallaste	Kallas Krasnaja Gora	Rakvere	Wesenberg
Karksi-Nuia	Karkus-Nuia	Rapla	Rappel

NEW	OLD	NEW	OLD
Kehra	Kedder (Jaunack)	Räpina	Rappin
Keila	Kegel	Saue	Klein-Sauss Friedrichshof
Kilingi-Nõmme	Kurkund-Nõmme	Sillamäe	Bruggen Türsel
Kiviõli	Erra-Sala Kiviõli	Sindi	Zintenhoff
Kohtla-Järve	Kohtel	Suure-Jaani	Gross-Johannis
Kunda	Kunda	Tallinn	Reval
Kuressaare	Arensburg Kingissepa	Tamsalu	Tamsal
Kärdla	Kertel (Kertelhof)	Tapa	Taps
Lihula	Leal	Tartu	Dorpat
Loksa	Loksa	Tõrva	Tõrwa
Maardu	Maart	Türi	Turgel
Mustvee	Tschorna	Valga	Walk
Mõisaküla	Moiseküll Latvian=Platera	Viljandi	Fellin
Narva	Narva	Võhma	Wechma
Narva-Jõesuu	Hungerburg	Võru	Werro
Otepää	Odenpäh		

Part of a list of birth records for Voru (Werro) and Tartu (Yuriev) were published in the Latvia SIG Newsletter; Volume 5-Issue 2 of May 2000 pages 19-23. The information was submitted by Len Yodaiken. Back copies may be ordered if available from the Latvia SIG Treasurer.

ARCHIVES AND RESOURCES

Estonian History Archives (EHA) - Eesti Ajalooarhiiv,
Liivi 4, Tartu 50409, Estonia
Tel: +372 7 387 500 - Fax: +372 7 387 510
Web site: <http://www.ra.eha.ee>

Estonia State Archives (ESA) - Eesti Riigiarhiiv,
Maneezi, 4, Tallinn 15019, Estonia
Tel: +372 693 8111 – Fax: +372 661 6230
Web site: <http://www.ra.gov.ee>
E-mail: riigiarhiiv@ra.ee

Tallinn City Archives (TCA)
Tallinna Linnaarhiiv
Tolli Tanav 6, 10133 Tallinn, Estonia
Fax: +372 645 7401   Fax: +372 645 7400
E-mail: arhiiv@ tla.ee
Web site: <http://www.tallinn.ee>

The Estonian History Archives (EHA), Tartu and the Estonian State Archives (ESA) in Tallinn were united into the Estonian National Archives in 1999 but remain at their original premises. Most material of interest to Jews is kept at both the EHA and ESA.

National Archives of Estonia (Rahvusarhiiv)
J. Liivi 4, Tartu 50409, Estonia
Tel: +372 7 387 505
Fax: +372 7 387 514
E-mail: rahvusarhiiv@ra.ee

Archives of the Association of Latvian & Estonian Jews in Israel. See page 22

State Historical Archives (Ajalooarhiiv)
Juhan Liivi 4, 202400 Tartu, Estonia

Estonian Records held in Latvian State Historical Archives in Riga[17]

PLACE	DISTRICT	PROVINCE	RECORDS
Dorpat (Tartu)	Dorpat (Tartu)	Livland (Estonia)	Vital records of the Jewish community of Riga 1880-1905
Fellin (Viljandi)	Fellin (Viljandi)	Livland (Estonia)	Estonia vital records of the Jewish community of Riga 1880-1905
Pernau (Pernava)	Pernau (Pernava)	Livland (Estonia)	Vital records of the Jewish community of Riga 1880-1905
Werro (Woro)	Werro (Woro)	Livland (Estonia)	Vital records of the Jewish community of Riga 1880-1905

Main Estonian resources in LDS centres[18]

When tracing Jewish roots in modern Estonia, the most valuable resource is the LDS films, which contain nearly all of the Jewish records for Estonian cities and towns. These films were made in 1994 by the LDS and are easily available in their Family History Centres, which are in most western countries except for Israel. Most of the original records were written in Russian and Hebrew, but from the 1920s they were written in Estonian and in some cases even German paired with Hebrew. The records cover the period from 1872 to 1940, but it is only for Tallinn that records exist for all those years. For the smaller towns you only find records for shorter periods.

Most Estonian towns were previously situated in the Lifland Gubernia, which was part of the Riga Rabbinate, so many births, marriages, divorces and deaths for these towns were listed in the Riga metrical books. Some of the LDS records are excerpts from the Riga books. This is, for example, the situation with the Võru records for the years 1883-1925. So, if you do not find your relatives in the Estonian LDS-films, they may be listed in the Riga books found in the Latvian State Historical Archives in Riga.

THE LDS-FILMS

There are four LDS-films containing Jewish records from modern Estonia.

Film 1921257:

1	Tallinn: Deaths 1936-40: in Estonian
2	Rakvere: Births, marriages and deaths 1921-26: in Estonian and Hebrew
3-6	Tartu: Births, marriages and deaths 1906: In Russian
7-45	Tartu: Births, marriages, divorces and deaths 1907-17: in Russian and Hebrew
46-49	Tartu: Births, marriages, divorces and deaths 1918: in German and Hebrew
50-53	Tartu: Births, marriages, divorces and deaths 1919: in Russian and Hebrew
54-56	Tartu: Births, marriages, divorces and deaths 1920: in German and Hebrew

Film 1921258:

1-18	Tartu: Births, marriages, divorces and deaths 1921-26: in Estonian and Hebrew
19	Tartu: Births, marriages, divorces and deaths 1897-1926: in Russian, Hebrew and Estonian: Excerpts of the original records.
20	Valga: Births, marriages and deaths 1919-25: in Russian and Estonian
21-22	Viljandi: Births, marriages and deaths 1917-26: in Russian
23	Võru: Births 1883-1925: In Russian: Excerpts from the original records
24	Võru: Deaths 1918-26: In Russian

Film 1921300:

1-28	Narva: Births, marriages, divorces and deaths 1911-26: in Russian
29	Rakvere: Births, marriages and deaths 1921-26: in Estonian and Hebrew
30	Tallinn: Births 1872-75: in Russian
31	Tallinn: Births 1877: in Russian
32	Tallinn: Births, marriages, divorces and deaths 1878: in Russian and Hebrew
33-46	Tallinn: Births, marriages, divorces and deaths 1879-87: in Russian and Hebrew
47	Tallinn: Deaths 1890-1914 and births 1890-95: in Russian and Hebrew

Film 1921301:

1-2	Tallinn: Births 1896-1919, divorces 1890-1914, deaths 1890-1919 and marriages 1915-19: in Russian and Hebrew
3	Tallinn: Births, marriages and deaths 1917-23: in Russian, Estonian and Hebrew
4	Tallinn: Birth certificates 1920-26: in Russian and Estonian
5	Tallinn: Births, marriages, divorces and deaths 1925-26: in Estonian and Hebrew
6-8	Tallinn: Births 1926-40, marriages 1926-38 and deaths 1926-36

OTHER LDS-FILMS

There are also many other LDS films containing records from Estonia, but of course many of them show Christian church records.

There are censuses for some cities and towns in the LDS registers called "Seelen-revision". These records go back to the 17th century for Tallinn, the 18th century for other towns in Estonia, and up to the early 20th century. Jews may appear here in separate lists. The cities and town represented are:

Pärnu: 1795-1888
Rakvere: 1795-1900
Tallinn: 1689-1908
Tartu: 1799-1907
Valga: 1795-1914
Viljandi: 1782-1916

Education

Jewish Schools[19]

In the second half of the 19th century Jewish communities were spreading in the provinces of Livonia and Estonia. The Jewish community of Tallinn was allowed to hire a schoolmaster in 1864 and a special school commission was founded at the office of the General Governor to run the Jewish schools in Curonia (Courland). 81 Jewish children were studying at schools in Curonia in 1824-1825 and this is the oldest data on the organisation of Jewish educational life in the Baltics.

EHA Fond 384

From the correspondence between the Curator and the Russian Minister of Education one can reconstruct the activities and organisation of the Jewish schools in Livonia from 1844 to 1900. In the fond named the "The Directorate of the schools of Tartu" there is material relating to the Jewish schools in Tartu between 1876 and 1885.

EHA Fond 386

Higher education of Jews

Fond 404 (1848-1918)	University of Tartu
Fond 404 (1848-1918)	Veterinary Institute of Tartu
Fond 1734 (1907-1920)	Private university courses of Prof M Rostovtsev

There are very important personal files of Jewish students up to the year 1891. From 1893 to 1944 there are also biographical data, photos, scholarship requests, etc.

EHA Fond 402

Russian legislation had special requirements for acceptance, registration and examination of Jewish students from 1888 to 1917. The acceptable quota was 3%-10%, but at the end of the 1890s 18%-20% of students were Jewish. This was because of special applications from the Minister of Public Education and the Curator of Tartu University. Jewish students were not allowed to marry.

EHA Fond 402

Jewish student fraternities were founded in the 1880s. The EHA (Estonian History Archive) has collections of the following organisations:

The Scientific Society of History and Literature (1883-1916)
The Jewish Treasury of Mutual Aid (1883-1916)
The Society of Literature and Music (1892-1916)

EHA Fond 402

The University of Tartu has collections of the following organisations:

The Jewish Student Treasury
The Academic Jewish Society of Literature and History (1918)
The Academic Society for Jewish History and Culture (1920 – 1941)
The Society of Jewish Female Students Hacfiro (1925-1938)
The Academic Jewish Society Limuwia (1940)
The Academic Society for the Studies of Judaism Shatal (1932 -1939)

EHA Fond 2100

The ESA (Estonian State Archives) in Tallinn also has many other documents relating to Jewish students
ESA Fonds 2293 & 2296

There are records of the Jewish Cultural Boards of Trustees of Narva, Parnu, Tartu Valga, Viljandi and Voru-Petseri.

Latvia SIG has lists of Jewish students at the University of Tartu, 1889-1918. Until 1882 most of the students at Tartu University came from the province of Curonia (Courland). Jewish students were studying at Tartu from the first years after the re-establishment of the University by the Russian authorities in 1802. After the pogroms of 1881 the University received students from distant regions like Kiev. A Chair of Jewish Studies was founded in 1930. Prof Lazar Gulkowitsch came to the University in 1934 to become the Professor of Jewish Studies.

THE HOLOCAUST IN ESTONIA

In 1920 Estonia adopted a democratic constitution, which included a chapter on minority rights. Estonia was the most tolerant country in Eastern Europe between 1920 and 1934. A council of the Jewish community was elected in 1926, made up of 27 individuals with an Executive of seven persons. The Jewish National Foundation in Palestine awarded a 'Golden Book Certificate' to Estonia in 1927 for its tolerant and democratic treatment of minorities.[20]

There were 4,434 Jews in 1934. A coup d'état that year brought policies similar to those in Latvia and Lithuania whereby Jews were expelled from the free professions and were not granted licenses to operate businesses. There were unofficial quotas for universities and state jobs were barred.

A significant part of the repressive policy conducted in Estonia by Soviet occupation powers in 1940–88 was repression of individuals. People who were presumed to be disloyal to the regime vanished without trace (were secretly murdered) or were executed publicly without trial. Arrests for political reasons and deportations to distant Russian prison camps were carried out continuously. The deportations of June 1941 and March 1949 were both carried out in a massive sweep over a couple of days. In the former, more than 10,000 people had to leave their homes, and most were arrested and taken to prison camps, where probably as many as 95% of them perished. In 1949, 8,065 people of the 30,119 on the lists escaped.

Arrests and confiscation of property, and especially mass deportations and flight to the west, left furnished flats empty, which attracted Russian immigrants, whom the occupation powers imported in great numbers to join in the division of the spoils. Many continue using the property to the present day.

A general legal rehabilitation of the persons unjustly repressed for political reasons took place in 1989-1991. This allowed practically all deported persons or their heirs, as well as the heirs of the people who had been shot or died in prison camps, to be among those entitled to restitution of property. The progress of the actual process of restitution, however, is hampered by numerous restrictions.

BIBLIOGRAPHY FOR ESTONIA

Album Academicum Universitatis Tartueniis
(Academic album of Tartu University) 1918-1944. 3 Vols.
Amitan-Wilensky, Ella
Estonian Jewry - A Historical Summary; from M. Bobe, The Jews in Latvia. Tel Aviv: 1971
Dworzecki, M
Mahanoth HaYehudim beEstoniyah (The camps of the Jews in Estonia) 1970. With English summary
Genss, Nosen
Zur Geschichte fun der Juden in Livonia und Estland (History of the Jews in Livonia and Estonia) 2 Vols. 1933-1937, German
Genss, Nosen
Bibliografie fun Yidishe Druk-Oysgabn in Esti, 1937 (Bibliography of Yiddish publications in Estonia)
Gurin, Samuel
Statistics of the Jewish Population of Estonia
Juudi Kultuurvalitsuse väljaanne   Tallinn: 1936
Gurin-Loov, Eugenia
Holocaust of Estonian Jews, Tallinn: 1994, Estonian etc.
Jokton, K
Di Geshikhte fun di Yidn in Estland
(History of the Jews in Estonia) Tartu: 1927. Yiddish
Juudi Vahemusrahvuse Kultuuromavalitsuse Juubeli Album Tallinn 1926.
(The Jubilee Album of the Autonomous Cultural Administration of the Jews of Estonia)
Levin, Dov
Pinchas HaKehillot (History of the Communities)
Latvia and Estonia. Hebrew. Yad VaShem. Jerusalem: 1988
Levin, Dov
Estonian Jews in the USSR (1941-1945), Research based on survivors' testimonies, Yad VaShem Studies. Jerusalem: 1976

Martinson, E
Eesti Riklik Kirjastus Tallin 1962
(Estonia under the heel of the swastika) Estonia.
There is also a Russian Ed.

Nodel, Emanuel
Life and Death of Estonian Jewry, Baltic History, Cleveland
OH: 1973

Rabbi Menachem Barkahan
Latvia. Synagogues and Rabbis 1918–1940

Shor, Tatjana
'Judaica in the Historical Archives of Estonia'
Avoyaynu Vol. IX, *No. 4*. Pp. XXIII-XXIV Winter 1993

Yodaiken, Len
The Judeikin Family History and Tree, 1998, private edition
Pre-Independence Estonian Birth Documents,
Sharsheret HaDorot Vol. 12 *No. 2*. Pp. IX – XIII, June 1998

REFERENCES

[1] Extracts from text by Marger Vestermanis Director of the Jewish Museum in Riga. Fragments of the Jewish History of Riga

[2] Mike Getz

[3] Constance Whippmann

[4] Notes from Anna Olswanger

[5] Rita Bogdanova Latvian State Historical Archives

[6] Marion Werle Latvia SIG Webpage

[7] Vlad Soshnikov Notes from lecture at 20th International Conference for Jewish Genealogy in Salt Lake City July 2000

[8] Aleksandrys Feigmanis Latvia SIG Newsletter Vol 3, Number 3. September 1998

[9]   Rita Bogdanova Latvian State Historical Archives

[10]   Vlad Soshnikov Notes from lecture at 20th International Conference for Jewish Genealogy in Salt Lake City July 2000

[11]   Nick Evans The Port Jews of Libau, 1880-1914
David Cesarani and Gemma Romain (eds.),
Jews and Port Cities, 1590-1990: Commerce, Community and Cosmopolitanism (Vallentine Mitchell, 2006),
pp.197-214

[12]   Latvia SIG Newsletter Vol 3, Number 4 December 1998

[13]   Vadim Altskan United States Holocaust Museum Washington DC

[14]   Latvia on the Web Joseph Gar. The Holocaust in Latvia

[15]   Toomas Hiio Jewish Students and Jewish Organisations at University of Tartu Annual report 1998 Tartu History Museum

[16]   Dr. Tatjana Schor Avotaynu Vol 9, No 3 1993

[17]   Rita Bogdanova Latvian State Historical Archives

[18]   Adam Katzeff

[19]   Dr. Tatjana Schor Sources in Estonia for Jewish Education History. Annual report 1998 Tartu History Museum

[20]   Prof Aivars Stranga Jewish communities in the Baltic States 1918-1940. Paper given at Conference Jews in a Changing World.

INDEX

140

PUBLICATIONS
IN THE 'JEWISH ANCESTORS' SERIES

Jewish Ancestors?
A Guide to Jewish Genealogy in Germany and Austria
ISBN: 0 9537669 1 8
Written by: Thea Skyte and Randol Schoenberg
Series Editor: Rosemary Wenzerul
◆ An insight into researching your Germany or Austrian family roots◆
◆An informative guide to the archives of available records◆
◆Explains how to obtain the records you thought no longer existed◆
Price: £4.50 + 50p p&p (U.K) and £6.00/US$10 (Overseas)

Jewish Ancestors?
A Guide to Jewish Genealogy in the United Kingdom
ISBN: 0 9537669 7 7
Contributing Editor: Rosemary Wenzerul
◆ Information on Jewish holdings of resource centres throughout the UK◆
◆All information and bibliography presented by Town◆
◆All UK Jewish cemeteries listed◆
◆Ideal for beginners and experienced genealogists and overseas visitors to the UK◆
Price: £5.95 + 80p p&p (U.K) and £8.95 (US$16) (Overseas)

Jewish Ancestors?
A Guide to Organising Your Family History Records
ISBN: 0 9537669 4 2
Written by: Rosemary Wenzerul
◆If your papers are in a mess then this book is for you◆
◆Are your records suitably preserved for future generations? ◆
◆Up to date information about new technology◆
◆Hundreds of ideas to help you◆
Price: £4.95 + 80p p&p (U.K) £6.95 p&p (US$13) (Overseas)

143